I Am
With You
Always

Meeting Jesus
in Every Season of Life

Gerrit Scott Dawson

PLC Publications

I Am With You Always

Meeting Jesus in Every Season of Life

© 2000 Gerrit Scott Dawson

PLC Publications
PO Box 2210
Lenoir, NC 28645

Book design by Paula R. Kincaid

Cover design by PrintSystems, Inc.

First printing

ISBN 0-9652602-8-3

Library of Congress Catalog Card Number 00-134411

PRINTED IN THE UNITED STATES OF AMERICA

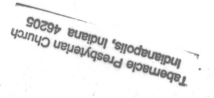
For Leah
Who Lives the Ministry of Presence.

Contents

PREFACE   vii

CHAPTER ONE   1
Come to Me – *Matthew 11:28-30*

CHAPTER TWO   9
The Father and the Son – *Matthew 11:25-30*

CHAPTER THREE   17
Even Years Down the Wrong Road – *Luke 5:27-32*

CHAPTER FOUR   27
Not Distracted by Externals – *Luke 7:1-10*

CHAPTER FIVE   37
In the Midst of Loss – *Luke 7:11-17*

CHAPTER SIX   47
When We Are Being Torn Apart – *Luke 8:26-39*

CHAPTER SEVEN   57
Even If We Are Too Little, Too Late – *Matthew 14:13-21*

CHAPTER EIGHT   65
On the Contrary Night Seas – *Matthew 14:22-36*

CHAPTER NINE   75
   Along the Way – *Mark 8:27-38*

CHAPTER TEN   85
   In a Shining Moment – *Mark 9:2-13*

CHAPTER ELEVEN   95
   Asking What We Want – *Luke 18:35-42*

CHAPTER TWELVE   103
   Seeking What Was Lost – *Luke 19:1-10*

CHAPTER THIRTEEN   111
   In the Hour of Betrayal – *Luke 22:31-32*

CHAPTER FOURTEEN   119
   Words from the Cross – *Luke 23:26-43*

CHAPTER FIFTEEN   129
   In the Turning of the Tears – *John 20:10-18*

CHAPTER SIXTEEN   141
   I Am With You Always – *Matthew 28:16-20*

Preface

This is a "friends" book. It tugged at me when I saw my beloved secretary, Evelyn Creason, looking for a book she could give to a friend going through a rough time. I thought then, "I wish I had a book about Jesus that you could give people for various situations in life."

The opportunity came when my friend, Richard Fisher, of the Bible Reading Fellowship in Oxford, asked me if I would write a book for them. He knew I was on a break from new projects; he also knew I was waiting eagerly for God to send direction. At the time, our family was enjoying the marvelous hospitality of friends: the Ben Johnstone family and their congregation in Mallaig, Scotland. Spending the summer in their home overlooking the Sound of Sleat and the Isle of Skye, it wasn't hard to be inspired.

As the work progressed, it seemed fitting to offer the manuscript to my friend and colleague Parker Williamson, in hopes of furthering the mission of the Presbyterian Lay Committee, and I'm thankful the board chose to publish it.

The whole substance of the book, however, would have been impossible without the prior work of some great theologians who have, beyond hope, invited me into the sphere of their friendship: Thomas, James and Alan Torrance and Douglas Kelly live the love of the Christ they proclaim.

So, now it's in your hands. I pray that you will meet Jesus in its pages, whatever season of life you're in. And it would be just great if you were moved to pass it along to a friend, too.

CHAPTER ONE

Come to Me

Matthew 11:28-30

Come to me, all you who are weary
and burdened, and I will give you rest.

Matthew 11:28

He came to us with an invitation. The Son of God stooped so low as to be joined with human flesh, limiting himself to the world of dust and swiftly passing time – in order to give us a personal appeal. "Come to me." Jesus made the first move, crossing the divide between God and humanity, showing us his very heart. And his word to a weary, burdened people was "Come to me and I will give you rest."

Once, I led a Bible study group in which I asked people to choose a one or two word description for the current state of their lives. More than half chose some form of "Stressed Out." And when I asked what phrase they wished they could choose instead, these same people replied, "Peaceful." Perhaps you, too, would have nodded in agreement. We are a restless people, unable to get out from under the daily demands that weigh us down from dawn to midnight. We do not know how to still the wanting, wandering heart within that never quite knows what it wants except that it must be something other than what it has.

I remember watching my younger son opening his Christmas presents when he was 15 months old. He was as interested in the wrapping paper as the presents themselves. And he was in no hurry to move on. "Let's shake this box. And let's taste that ribbon!" But the rest of us had gifts to open, and dinners to attend. We began shoving presents toward the child who was contentedly absorbed in trying to encompass the nose of a large stuffed animal with his own tiny mouth. "Poor guy," I thought, "You'll learn soon enough to be like the rest of us – always on to the next thing." And he did.

"Come to me," said Jesus, "All you who are weary and burdened, and I will give you rest." It's such a personal invitation. He seems to know us just as we are, as if to say, "I know you're tired from life in this world. I understand that you're burdened by expectations. Perhaps you think you are alone, cut off from God and sent to carry on as best you can on your own. I know. Come to me and I will give you rest. You will see that you are never alone. Learn from me, for I am gentle and you will find rest for your souls."

A great theologian has said that nowhere is God's supreme greatness so clearly seen than in the gentleness with which he approaches us in Jesus. Only the Almighty could come casting aside all trappings of royalty to issue this humble invitation. He asks us to come to him when he himself has already come all the way to where we are. And he continues to arrive on the threshold of our hearts in every stage and situation of life. Jesus invites us to look up for a moment from the burdens of the day and see him waiting for us with open arms. Of course he could overwhelm our frail frames with one breath. But the Son of God is gentle and humble of heart. He comes to us, and then he waits for us to turn to him.

Sources of weariness

Jesus knew that his people were burdened. As we think about their lives, we may identify three sources of their weariness, and then make comparisons with today. First, daily life in itself was demanding. The people worked as fishers, farmers, shepherds and merchants. They lived close to the land and sea, working hard to gather meager fruit from constant labor. Technology and medical care were primitive. Life-spans were short. Pain was simply part of being alive.

The people in Jesus' day bore a heavy load just to get by. But the second weariness arose from the reality that they were no longer a free people. Rome ruled the country. The days of independence for the people of God were long gone, kept alive only in the hopes for a Messiah, and the covert schemings of rebel groups. They knew themselves to be subjects. And for all the order and stability the Romans supposedly brought, there were heavy taxes to pay. Many independent farmers had lost their lands and become tenants. A nation that had once flourished with its own culture and wealth was now a remote outpost providing a stream of revenue to the emperor in Rome.

But even this could have been borne had the people not experienced the third source of weariness. They felt cut off from their God. The influential religious leaders known as the Pharisees had arisen as a group dedicated to preserving the faith of Israel amidst the force of cultural absorption by Rome. By meticulously keeping the law, they held onto their identity as God's people, and kept alive the hope that God would one day remember Israel and restore their nation. But along the way they had distorted the law of God as they added more duties to "hedge" the law so that one would not even come close to disobeying it. Then, they turned their observances into a legalism to be imposed on others.

The average person had no chance of maintaining such standards of purity. Not only did the people have to bear the sense of judgment that Roman rule brought, but they had to relate to God under a continuing message that they were spiritually unclean and therefore unworthy to approach a holy God. Into this atmosphere, Jesus came with his loving invitation.

The weight of everyday

We, too, know what it is to be weary from the demands of daily life. I imagine a woman who looks in the mirror and notices the lines of care, even as she remembers how smooth and creamy that face had been, not so very long ago. She rises early, always before she has had enough sleep, to dress, make lunches, and get the others out the door on time. Work is demanding but the compensation is never enough. She manages, though, to keep her job in its own compartment. For after work there are practices and meetings, and her own aged mother to check on. No matter how modern her family may seem, the usual preparation of dinner and keeping up the house fall to her. It is late before she finally falls into bed, still feeling behind.

There is also tiredness that comes from working for someone who holds tremendous power over our well-being. I imagine a man who feels the pressure to perform at work day after day, and perhaps feels just a measure short all the time. He's worked his way from the bottom to the middle. He has come to realize that he probably won't go much higher. He can reconcile himself to that reality, but he is terrified of where he might fall. In a heartbeat, he could be replaced with someone younger, quicker, cheaper. And he knows his life is not his own. The mortgage on the house has a long way to go. He didn't mean to get further into debt, but the remodeling had to be done and now the kids seem to need more and more all the time. This man can't stop; he can't get sick; he must stay at it. Too many people require something from him. Rome rules, though it has taken a new name. And this man is so tired.

In the midst of such pressures, we would hope that people could find a source of strength in God. But all too often, we labor under the third source of weariness just as ancient Israel did. We feel cut off from God because we cannot measure up to his standards. Somehow, we have accepted the mistaken notion that God's attitude toward us begins with a huge IF. "*If* you keep all my commands, *if* you go to church all the time, *if* you pray like a saint, *if* you are good and don't do what you want to do but always just do religious things, *if* you do all of that, then I will love you and bless you." Under such conditions, we have to feel that God's basic disposition toward us is displeasure. God has to be against us, because we can never be (in fact we don't even want to be) the holy, spiritual people we think God requires.

In this kind of thinking, we are left on our own. Since God must not want anything we want, it's up to us to build our lives and pursue our own fulfillment. Even Christians join the culture in the restless quest to fill our emptiness with satisfying experiences. Though we know better in our souls, we buy into the illusion that we actually can attain what we need. So, we quest after the next holiday abroad, the new accolade at work, the achievement of our children, the purchase of the right piece of furniture, the savoring of the latest restaurant. Each provides a temporary satisfaction. We receive a momentary ease for our lonely, restless lives. But then, like my son at Christmas, we're pushed on to the next thing.

And there may seem to be no way off this road along which everyone rushes. God must be against us, since we have been so unreligious in our pursuits and fulfilled so few of his supposed conditions. We're worn out, but we can't stop. Banks and businesses, media and personal expectations seem to have us on a forced march. We just can't keep up anymore, but we don't know another way.

The yoke that eases our burden

To us Jesus speaks softly, in a voice that penetrates our desperation with a calming tone, "Come to me, all you who are weary and heavy laden, and I will give you rest." God is not against us, but for us! He has come to us in Jesus Christ offering what we long for: rest, the sense of peace, the underlying assurance that all is well and we are kept in loving arms.

Jesus speaks to those who bear so many burdens of responsibility, and goes on to say, "Take my yoke upon you and learn from me, for I am gentle and humble in heart, and you will find rest for your souls. For my yoke is easy and my burden is light" (Matt. 11:29-30). A yoke is a frame used to connect a pair of working animals to each other and the burden they are pulling. It can also be the frame a person would carry over the shoulders with a bucket or sack balanced on each end. Yokes, therefore, have long been a symbol of service. A man in my congregation suggested how interesting it is that Jesus, the son of a carpenter, used this image. Wooden yokes in those days would have been individually made to suit the unique shape of the animals doing the work. With a good fit, chaffing and discomfort would be prevented while efficiency would be increased. The carpenter would understand the difference between a yoke that made every step an agony and a yoke which enabled the animal to do the work the day required.

We all wear the yoke that links us to the responsibilities and demands of the daily world. Often, this yoke becomes a symbol of our weariness. Jesus tells us that God has a new yoke for us to wear. It involves a new field for us to follow and a new direction for us to tread. Yes, it is a burden to turn around in our lives and come to Jesus. But Jesus' tender assurance is that his yoke will not be too difficult. It will fit comfortably. Jesus' way will feel like the life we have always wanted to live, the road we have always dreamed we should walk. His burden is not heavy because it is the one we were made to bear. In fact, in taking his yoke, we will be linked to him and all he has to give us.

In Jesus' invitation we may hear that we were never meant to go it alone in this hard life. God's disposition toward us is fundamentally one of invitation and love. We need no longer travel along the exhausting highway of trying to make our lives work on our own. The culture may tell us that such self-pursuit is freedom, but we may know the truth now. Being alone, cut off from God, is the worst kind of slavery. For then we cannot get out of ourselves. And so our weary souls can never find rest. But now there is a way home. "Come to me," says Jesus, "Learn from me."

We may come home to Jesus because he has first come all the way down to where we are. Now we may turn to him because he is not far removed from us in a cloud of disapproving holiness. He is here. His arms are open in welcoming acceptance. The Son of God has come so close to the world he loves that he has actually taken to himself our skin and bones. Experiencing our weariness from within a human body, he knows the burdens we bear. Jesus entered our lost and exhausted condition. From the inside out, he has felt in his body our tiredness and seen with human eyes the loneliness in our eyes. He came so close that we could actually smell the dust of travel on his robes and hear the tenor of his voice. From the position of being among us, Jesus invites us to turn to him and find rest.

This does not mean that Jesus promises that the burdens of life will disappear. Turning toward him may mean no change in the difficult external circumstances of our lives. What he offers is a peace in the soul that enables us to have strength to carry on. As we learn from him, we begin to see purpose and meaning even in the midst of suffering. Life takes on a larger, deeper perspective. And best of all, in a most profound way, we learn that we are not alone. We are with him, and he is with us. Jesus brings life in abundance, and his vivid presence lifts us out of ourselves and so lifts our weariness.

This book is meant to help us answer Jesus' invitation. He implores us to come and learn from him. So we will turn our attention towards Jesus as we consider a series of stories from the gospels. We will consider accounts of how Jesus came to people in every situation of life with his gentle, humble heart continually offering his gracious love. And we will look at significant events from Jesus' own life to see how even in his suffering he gave himself to us. In each case, we will try to make the connection between the people of Jesus' day and our lives now. I invite you to take on the yoke of turning towards Jesus through considering these stories with an expectant heart. "Come to me," he says. As you turn the pages in this book, join me in replying, "I'm here, Lord. Let me learn from you."

————— • ———

O Lord, as you name our weariness, we become aware of how tired we have been carrying the burdens of this life. As you invite us to come to you, our hearts flicker with hope that we need no longer live as if it is all on us. We turn, daring to imagine that you might lift us into strong, loving arms. Restore us, gracious Jesus, with your love. Place upon us the yoke that fits, the yoke of living in step with you. Amen.

CHAPTER TWO

The Father and the Son

Matthew 11:25-30

*All things have been committed to me by my
Father. No one knows the Son except the Father,
and no one knows the Father except the Son and
those to whom the Son chooses to reveal him.*

Matthew 11:27

A story is told of the days when the great Scottish theologian
Thomas F. Torrance served as a chaplain in northern Italy during
the second World War. He came to a young soldier who had been
wounded and knew he would soon die there on the battlefield. As
Torrance tried to comfort him, the soldier asked a question with
great urgency: "When I meet God, will he be like Jesus? Will he
be like the Jesus I have heard about in Sunday school or someone
else?" Though he was years away from writing the books in
which he would answer that question with deep theological elo-
quence, Torrance was able to reply with confidence, "Yes, God
will be exactly like Jesus." The young man died comforted.

When we hear the gracious welcome, "Come to me," we are
led to consider just who is this man who issues the profound invitation to find rest in his presence. Hearing him, are we hearing
distinctly the very voice of God? Seeing him, are we gazing into
the heart of his Father? To answer such questions, we may look
back in Matthew 11 and ponder the words Jesus spoke just before

he offered rest to the weary. We will see that Jesus was conclud-
ing a rather long discourse that took several turns of thought and
feeling. By following Jesus' words, we may see more clearly both
the passions and the primary relationship which shaped Jesus'
invitation to us.

From reproach to praise

Jesus' cousin, John the Baptist, had been imprisoned by King
Herod. Prior to his arrest, John had been out in the wilderness by
the banks of the Jordan River preaching a message of repentance
in preparation for the coming of God's Messiah. From jail, John
sent word by his disciples asking Jesus if he were indeed the
expected Christ. Jesus replied by pointing to his works: "The blind
receive sight, the lame walk, those who have leprosy are cured …
and the good news is preached to the poor" (Matt. 11:5). These
were the Old Testament signs of the promised Redeemer's works.

Jesus went on, however, to discuss John with the assembled
crowd. He hailed him as a great prophet, even asserting that
"among those born of women there has not risen anyone greater
than John the Baptist" (Matt. 11:11). We know that vast numbers
went out to hear John and were baptized by him. But either not
enough went or the message did not take with those who did hear
him. For Jesus next decried the lack of acceptance of both John
and himself. He was scathing in his remarks, comparing the people to petulant children who would not be pleased with anything
offered to them.

Then, Jesus denounced the cities where he had performed
miracles for their refusal to repent in the face of God's evident
activity among them. In a chilling review, Jesus said that the fate
of Sodom, notorious even today for its wickedness, would be
more bearable than the judgment awaiting the cities that had seen
him but not believed. Even the rich, self-sufficient Gentile cities
of Tyre and Sidon would have turned to God upon seeing his
works, said Jesus, but the cities of God's own people had not
responded. Following this flow of thought, it is hard to imagine
Jesus would conclude with the comforting words we considered
in the last chapter.

Abruptly, though, Jesus changed course. He turned from the crowd and raised his voice in prayer. His tone changed from bracing, perhaps lamenting, judgment to thanksgiving. "I praise you, Father, Lord of heaven and earth, because you have hidden these things from the wise and learned, and revealed them to little children. Yes, Father, for this was your good pleasure" (Matt. 11:25-26). The warning had been issued in striking enough terms that even those who needed a slap in the face to wake up would understand. There could be no claim that he wasn't clear.

But that given, Jesus could then rejoice that a plan that pleased his Father was being enacted. The "wise and learned," perhaps those who relied too much on their own cleverness or sophistication in thought, were not able to perceive who was before them. By contrast, Jesus gave thanks that the "little children" *were* getting it. The babes, those open-hearted and open-minded enough to be receptive, were realizing who Jesus was. In other words, those who felt sufficient in themselves resisted Jesus' intrusion into their world. But those who were willing to recognize their need were joyfully seeing how Jesus was the very one for whom they had longed.

The key here is not that Jesus was glad that the intellectuals were not receiving him. His long, strident descriptions of how people had refused to see were meant to rouse them. The very intensity of his denunciations indicated how much it mattered to him that people were missing the chance to embrace the life he offered. The reason for his joy, however, was that those who were needy and open were indeed coming to him. So, the power structures of the world were being overturned. The swift, the strong, the ruling, and the intelligentsia may have been first in that culture, but not in the kingdom of God. The fringe people, the broken, and the outsiders were coming into God's realm with abandon. They could see while others, blinded by their self-sufficiency, could not. And it gave Jesus joy to see such little ones coming to him for healing and rest.

A look behind the veil

Then, in one of the most sparkling passages in the New

Testament, Jesus pulled back the curtain so we could glimpse something of the inner life of God. "All things have been committed to me by my Father. No one knows the Son except the Father, and no one knows the Father except the Son and those to whom the Son chooses to reveal him" (Matt. 11:27).

In calling God his Father, Jesus was assuming an intimacy with God that was unheard of in his time. There could be no mistake. "I praise you Father, Lord of heaven and earth…" The one he addressed so intimately was the Sovereign God. And Jesus was saying that he is uniquely the Son of that Father. Two thousand years of Christianity later, we are apt to miss how important this is.

The very heart of who Jesus is may be found in this expression of the intimate relationship between the Father and the Son. The Father knows the Son – in such a deep, continuing way that they may be said to be one. The Son knows the Father – so thoroughly that he can make the Father known to others. This bond of active knowing tells us who God is, and who he is not. God is not just a big force that runs through everything. We know this now because we see in Jesus' words that the God of the universe is personal. God is not just spiritual energy, or some kind of world-consciousness. He is a God in relationship. He carries on his very being in this constant relationship between the Father and the Son. So, God is not a solitary, brooding oneness of judgment and law. We learn through Jesus that God is love. As the Son comes among us, we see God revealed. He turns his face toward us, and that countenance is shining with love. Paul tells us that we can see the glory of God shining in the face of Jesus (II Cor. 4:6) and Hebrews tells us that Jesus the Son is "the radiance of God's glory and the exact representation of his being, sustaining all things by his powerful word" (Heb. 1:3). In Jesus, we see who God is and that is tremendously good news, because Christ shows us how very much God is love, both within himself and toward us.

The Son does what he sees

Jesus said that the Father had committed "all things" to him. That phrase is so all-inclusive that we have to pause to consider what he might have meant. In sending the Son into the world as a human being, the Father was entrusting him with a mission. Jesus came to enact the love of God for the world. The Father committed the welfare of every human being to the Son. Jesus came to gather home the lost sons of Adam and the wandering daughters of Eve. He walked among us bearing the weight of the world on his shoulders. Upon him was the responsibility and the authority for establishing the salvation of humankind. Quite a trust!

In the gospel of John, Jesus illumined this further when he said, "I tell you the truth, the Son can do nothing by himself; he can do only what he sees his Father doing, because whatever the Father does, the Son also does. For the Father loves the Son and shows him all he does" (John 5:19-20). Perhaps human comparisons can help us understand this. Though too few of us had the relationships with our fathers for which we long, we may yet have a memory, or at least a dream, that will help us connect with Jesus' words.

Can you remember a time as a child when your father showed you something he was doing? Perhaps you were in the workshop, and he showed you how he was cutting a piece of wood. It was more than the mere granting of observation. He took the time to show you so you understood the secrets of how the tools worked. Or perhaps it was a time he took you on his lap and shared with you his plans – his vision for the garden or his dreams for career. He let you in on the mystery of what fathers are thinking about as they care for the family. Perhaps there was a time when your father showed you a trick with a rubber band, a shortcut in subtraction, a flower he had grown, a constellation in the night sky, the meaning of a word, or the way to throw a ball. Perhaps it was the first time you were old enough to be let in on his fears and worries.

When we were invited in to what our fathers were doing, we felt so loved and special. The memories, the precious few memories, are enough to bring even hardened adults to tears. Even the pain and anger of never knowing such loving moments make us realize how deeply rooted is our longing to know and be known by our fathers. These feelings perhaps, give us a taste of the intimacy Jesus described: The Father loves the Son and shows him all that he does.

I once discovered in a book a tiny painting which poignantly evokes this close relationship between the activity of the Father and the Son. In the middle ages, the manuscripts of sacred texts were often lavishly "illuminated" by painting pictures within the beginning letters of a chapter. In one 13th-century Psalter from France, within a letter "O," there is a depiction of Jesus on the cross. That in itself is not unusual except that behind the cross is the Father, sitting on a low throne. His arms are outstretched and he holds the ends of the horizontal beam in either hand. The vertical beam of the cross is planted between the Father's feet, so that the head of the suffering Son is right below the head of the suffering Father. The body of the Son is before the Father's chest and is thus at the heart of his love. Jesus said the Son does only what he sees his Father doing. If the Son allowed himself to be crucified, it was because the Father himself held the cross and suffered, too. This is the absolute oneness of knowing, seeing and doing that Jesus described as his relationship with his Father.

Crossing the divide

Another dimension Jesus' words reveal to us concerns the nature of this one who issues the invitation, "Come to me." He is both fully God and fully human. The man standing before the crowds saying, "No one knows the Father except the Son," spoke in a human voice. He stood a particular height and walked with a unique gait. He ate and slept, worked and grew tired as we do. Jesus was a man. Yet he also claimed that he had bridged the divide between flesh and spirit, the divine and human, this world and the spiritual realm. He knew the Father.

God is so infinitely greater and higher than we are that he cannot be known by us unless he chooses to reveal himself in ways we can comprehend. Jesus said that no one knows the Father – truly, intimately, completely knows him – except the Son, Jesus himself. Yet, Jesus had the authority and the ability to reveal the Father to others. He could make known the Father because he himself was the revelation of God to us. He was, and is, God come among us.

In other words, Jesus came from the heavenly realm to the earthly realm. He came in our form, as a human being. But in doing so he did not lose his intimate oneness with the Father. He remained the Son of God even as he assumed our frail humanity. So he lives in both realms, and, in fact, bridges in himself the gap between God and humanity. This is the import of his revealing the Father. In him, those to whom he makes known the Father are taken into the very communion of God, into the intimacy of the Father and the Son's relationship.

As the early Christians reflected on the oneness between Jesus the Son and his Father, they realized that a third divine person is involved as well, the Holy Spirit. The relationship that is God is not only two, but three persons in an ever loving, ever knowing, ever exchanging oneness. Even before there was a realm of time and space, of creatures and creation, there was God, living in a vibrant, exquisite communion of Father, Son and Holy Spirit. By recognizing the Triune being of God, we learn that when we see Jesus, we are seeing the Father. He is the exact representation of his Father. There is no God different from Jesus Christ. What we see Jesus to be, we may understand God the Father to be. So the ways in which Jesus comes to us in every season are the ways in which the very Triune God himself comes to us. Jesus is the revealing of God. The words to the soldier on the battlefield are addressed to us as well, "Yes, God is exactly like Jesus."

Our place

The news that Jesus proclaimed is that through him, the circle of oneness in the Triune God opens out now toward humanity. It is not closed, but open. Who may enter into this loving relationship? Jesus said that no one can know the Father except the Son and *those to whom the Son chooses to reveal him*. In other words, without the will of the Son, we cannot approach the Father. We do not have the capacity or the power. We don't have the reach to pull God down to us nor the standing to make a claim on him. We enter fellowship with him only if the Son, Jesus, chooses to make the Father known to us.

So the next question immediately arises: What about me? Does he choose me? Will he reveal the Father to me? Our answer comes in the very next words out of Jesus' mouth: "Come to me, *all* you who are weary ..." Only those to whom the Son chooses to reveal the Father can know him. And that Son says to the assembled crowd, Come to me, all. There is no exclusion. If you want to be invited you have been.

The distinction seems to be between the wise and learned, unrepentant and self-sufficient who will not come, and the little children, the weary and the burdened who welcome the invitation. The way into fellowship with the Triune God, then, is through our need, our burdens, our unraveling, our questions, our helplessness. We so often view our illnesses and our failures, our messes and our fears as negatives. But in truth they may be our teachers and guides. For whatever breaks down our human tendency toward independence from God can lead us to the Jesus who stands in our midst and says "Come to me." Self-sufficient and wise in our own eyes, we miss his appeal, and we will know him only as judge. But if we are wakened by his warning words or encouraged by his appeal to our tender, tired areas, we will find him a ready friend.

The rest of this book will consider the ways this extraordinary Jesus, this man who is God and God who is man, comes to us in every hour and circumstance of our lives. At all these junctures where weakness seems so glaring we may find opportunity to enter his fellowship, the fellowship of the Father and the Son in the Holy Spirit.

———————

G*racious Jesus, show us yourself; show us the Father! We would not let our self-sufficiency or pride keep us from you. Apart from you, we have no good. We long for your rest and peace. Oh, ever invite us to see the love of the Father shining in your face and speaking through your words, "Come to me." Amen.*

CHAPTER THREE

Even Years Down the Wrong Road

Luke 5:27-32

Follow me ... I have not come to call
the righteous, but sinners.

Luke 5:27, 31

One of the difficulties in accepting Jesus' invitation may be the sheer inertia of life. Many of us feel locked into our activities and can barely consider the possibility of change. On the Interstate of routine, the traffic is so thick and fast that most years we can't even switch lanes. We surely don't know how to get off the highway to go another direction. But in unguarded moments, while we fly along, the feeling may surface that the way things are isn't enough. Enough of what, we can't say. But there are gaps down in the soul, and the wind makes a draft through them as we speed through our days.

Sadly, so many compromises have been made, so many deals struck with our consciences and negotiations forged with our pasts, that we can hardly begin to describe what we're missing. We can't even say what we mean to each other. It feels too late to change. This is just the way things are. All we know how to do is to keep going with the routine. We pretend not to notice the heart-yearnings as we move through our paces. As a folk song has said, we just "nod over coffee," briefly acknowledging those who are important to us on our way out the door to the usual routine. We may secretly long for a different life, but because we don't know how to get one, or if it's even possible, we just keep on as we are.

Levi understood these feelings as he sat at his tax booth on the main road that went from the Mediterranean Sea past Capernaum, where Jesus had been teaching, all the way to Damascus. Levi was a man so compromised that he was locked into his life whether he wanted to be or not. His options were mortgaged to the hilt, and the spiritual creditors on either side of him were not inclined to refinance.

Levi was a Jewish man. Levi was a Roman tax collector. So, he was accepted by neither his own people nor his foreign employers. The Romans shrewdly sold the rights of tax collecting to locals. These tax franchises were lucrative business. The Romans told the collector what the assessment was, and after he met that figure, the rest was his. So the tax collector would make his profit by charging more than the already crushing Roman rate. The chariots and spears of Rome backed him against protest. Naturally his fellow Jews hated him. He had sold out to their pagan oppressors. Levi made a profit on the misery of his compatriots. But the Romans hated him, too. Though they ran the system, they despised a man so dishonorable that he would gouge his own people.

Ironically, Levi's name meant that his ancestry was in the Levite tribe, those people of Israel set aside by God for priestly service. The Levites owned no land but were to be supported by the tithes of the people. In return, they dedicated their lives to the service of the Lord's worship. The Levites maintained the continual sacrifices of atonement and thanksgiving. Through the Levites, reconciliation with God was effected. They served the Lord through the Temple worship on behalf of all the people. Now here was Levi living off the "offerings" of his people through the despised tax system. And in return, the people received from Levi not the joy of reconciled relations with God, but the misery of Roman servitude.

Levi, then, was rich, filthy rich, but isolated. He couldn't enjoy his wealth with those who had been family. He couldn't go to synagogue or to the Temple. And the Romans would never have him. His only friends were those like him, others who had compromised their heritage, their souls, their faith, their values until there was no turning back.

There were the prostitutes who had lost both virtue and the hope of family. Had they fled abuse? Had they been pushed against the wall because they were widowed or rejected and had no place to turn as women in that culture? Had their childhood innocence been bought and sold long before they ever had any choice? At least in the company of Levi and other sinners they could be who they were openly. And there were other corrupt business people. They had gotten rich with their shrewd swindling of common folk. Of course their souls had to be buried deep beneath the money in the process, but they tried not to think about that. They partied with Levi in the bizarre fellowship of those who had only the fruit of their lostness in common.

So Levi had a small circle of what he would have called friends. But trust was low and betrayal rampant. They were friends by default and need. Generally, he was a despised man, and no one hated him more than himself. Of course he didn't think about these things every day. He "nodded over coffee" like the rest of us, let the demands of the hour carry him to work, stayed late, and used whatever techniques he could to get to sleep at night.

The glorious interruption

But the gaps in his soul were still there. And when Jesus passed by, Levi felt a great wind rush through those holes. He realized in an instant how cold and exposed he was. But as his soul shivered, a warm voice beckoned him toward spring. "Follow me."

Two words. Two words, and suddenly a way out was opened up. No one had wanted anything from Levi, besides money, in years. No one ever willingly asked for *him* – for his company and his allegiance. "Follow me." Levi was immediately moved.

He recognized in Jesus another isolated soul. People like Levi have a sense for such things. Jesus hadn't been making friends among the officials in either Jerusalem or Rome. Polite society wouldn't have him. The religious leaders were intimidated by him and the common people were in awe. His few disciples hardly understood his mission. Though for entirely different reasons, Jesus, too, was essentially alone among people.

Yet Jesus, for all the loneliness and grief on his brow, also exuded a sense of deep, mature peace. There was life in him, welling up from a spring within. He radiated acceptance and love, even joy. Levi could always see that, too, because the presence of someone who had a fulfillment not tethered to circumstances awakened his hunger. He wanted what Jesus had desperately.

"Follow me." Follow him. Leave the tax booth unattended. Risk the wrath of Rome. Quit the job. Lose money. Go on the lam. Get out of town. Out of this prison. For what? For another start. For a new life. For a companionship not born of money, a fraternity made of people whose principal conversation was not how to keep the masses away from their assets and homes, but a fellowship based on the call of this man who had the audacity just to say, "Follow me."

In an instant Levi considered what it would be to have new conversations, to talk about God, to welcome others, to live for a purpose. Before he knew it, he stood up from his seat and went to Jesus. Someone had bought all the debts of his soul, paid off the spiritual creditors, and given him back his life. He had been compromised into a spiritual and social prison, but now the walls were torn down, and he was free again.

A new kind of party

Levi, though, did not liquidate everything right away. His connections to his old life did not just disappear. They also were transformed. He used his wealth to hold a great banquet for Jesus. Jesus' acceptance of him had opened the floodgates of gratitude. Levi invited everyone he knew. And as his house was grand, and the food and drink flowing, a great crowd of his old friends showed up. The other tax collectors came, as well as the prostitutes, the questionable business people, the hustlers, and the pretenders. All the compromised sinners showed up. And they had a great party. The wine ran and the food was magnificent. Jesus was there, and he didn't leave early. He loved them, and he feasted with them. His presence gave them a sense of being reconnected to life again.

This celebration, however, did not please the religious leaders of the day. The Pharisees had devoted their lives to purity. As we noted in the first chapter, these men had held fast to the faith of Israel amidst the pressures of Roman occupation and the temptations of the prevailing Greek culture. For God's people to survive, they believed, there could be no compromise over the law. Sadly, their pursuit of holiness all too often became a form of religious legalism that came out as judgment against more ordinary believers. They didn't care for this bash at Levi's house, and said to Jesus' disciples, "Why do you eat and drink with tax collectors and 'sinners'?" (Luke 5:30).

Jesus answered for his followers, "It is not the healthy who need a doctor, but the sick. I have not come to call the righteous, but sinners to repentance" (Luke 5:31-32). We may hear the similarity with his words in Matthew 11 when Jesus gave thanks that his identity was hidden from the "wise and learned" but made known to "little children." The strongest block to our reception of the Son of God who has come to us is not our sinfulness, but our refusal to admit it. Our compromises and brokenness, our poor choices and out-right destructiveness do not keep us from Jesus as surely as pretending we have no need of him. He has come for us, for those of us who will admit that we are not righteous – not right, not connected, not whole – but tired of life at this breakneck pace, and longing to be healed. He comes to answer our desperation with his forgiving, fulfilling presence.

So, Levi became one of the twelve. He has also been known as Matthew, and tradition assigns him authorship of the first gospel. Here, then is a story of a transformation greater even than physical healings.

And it is a story for all of us who know some secret tales of compromise in our lives. For example, have you ever started down a road thinking you'd just go that way for a while, and then found you couldn't get off, all these years later?

Have you held your tongue so long that you've forgotten what it is you needed to say, and fear now that if you opened your mouth the cries and the rage would blow down a house?

Have you ever pressed your lips against lips forbidden to you, and then not known how to stop, what to say, or how to look your spouse in the eye? Perhaps now the secret, long covered up, festers inside, poisoning your hours.

Have you gone along without truly dealing with important relationships until you realize you're just numb?

Have you ever rearranged the truth one time and then discovered how easy it is to do it another time, and another, and then found you could no longer tell right from wrong, fact from fiction, lies from truth?

Have you ever covered up, erased a figure, taken a life, hidden a diagnosis, passed the buck and the blame, looked the other way, held your tongue when you should have said something, or blurted out when you should have kept quiet? Have you ever worn a mask so long you began to believe it was really your face?

Oh yes, we have. Perhaps we haven't compromised ourselves in every one of these ways, but many of us have gone far enough down Levi's road that we understand. We know what it is to go to the tax booth every day, dancing on the edge of despair, nodding over coffee and hoping futilely that no winter wind will ever blow over our house of cards.

To all of us, Jesus says, "There's a way out. Follow me. You don't have to be imprisoned by what you've done or been. Follow me. I know who you are and I want you with me. I can pay your debts. Get up and let the coins fall into the dust, let the books flap in the wind, let the officials remind you of your contract. I can negotiate a new deal. No matter where you've been. No matter where you are. No matter how compromised your soul. No matter how soiled your hands. No matter how thick the prison walls seem. Follow me. I can get you out. I will set you free. Your life is with me now."

Jesus calls us. And from that moment, everything can change. With him there is forgiveness and grace. There is new life. Now, as immediately as he did to Levi, Jesus offers it to you.

The parties we may host

Of course there will still be the old life to deal with. But that suits Jesus fine. Levi held a party for Jesus and invited the only guests he knew: the tax collectors, the prostitutes and the rest of the sinners. And Jesus went and enjoyed the feast, partaking heartily. In that hour, Jesus not only rejoiced with Levi, but brought his love and joy to many others. The gospel got inside walls normally closed to religion. For Levi had access to people the Pharisees could never touch. He had connections with people who might think they could never get near Jesus. And Levi was not shy to tell them about what had happened to him. The old gaps in his soul were being filled. The long loneliness was over. His lies were finished and his prison gates were open. Life had begun again for Levi. As a result of his transformation, he could connect many others with this wonderful Jesus.

And that is precisely where you and I, as the compromised ones called by Jesus, have a mission to complete. There are people we may tell. We may invite others to join us in following the one who brings peace at last. Precisely because of our old compromises, we know people just like us. So we are able to enter places where others, who, thankfully, have been faithful and good for years, cannot go. The spiritual kinfolk of Levi can get into the board rooms and the staff meetings. We can reach the people out on the road. We can go into the shops, the factories, the warehouses, the stations. And to all those we may offer the words of life. We may bring them to a different kind of party, inviting them to join the fellowship of those who have answered Jesus' call.

Which church?

When I was at college, I alternated for a while between two churches (that is, when I went to church). I began at a beautiful church in the suburbs. Everything about it was perfect. The sanctuary was gorgeously appointed; the grounds were kept by a team of gardeners. All the people dressed beautifully. Success oozed from their smiles. The choir sounded like a heavenly host, and the minister preached doctrinally sound sermons with a smooth, rich voice. They seemed to do everything right. And that was the problem for me. Whenever I was there, I felt like scum. It was so perfect I couldn't stand it. Though of course the people may indeed have been loving and kind, I felt like I was so far beneath their notice that I could never be accepted.

I ended up at a church downtown. The inside was old and a bit musty, like the people. The choir wasn't as good. The preacher was all heart and his theology was a little loose. But there was an atmosphere there that I craved. It was said and understood and accepted that we were all sinners, looking for a word of grace. We were a ragtag lot, and generally astounded that Jesus called the likes of us. But he did, and we heard how much he loved us. And people looked at me as if I mattered to them.

I hope more of our churches will feel like that rickety downtown church than that perfect one. Our congregations need not be hesitant to declare openly that they are fellowships of lonely, compromised tax collectors being restored to life and love. That is far more important to an exhausted, despairing world than our hour of pretending everything is fine. Of course, I want our theology to be vigorous and sound, our choirs to make the angels rejoice, our people to be the best, sharpest and brightest disciples they can be. But always with the understanding that we are the brothers and sisters not of the Pharisees, but of Levi the tax collector and Mary the harlot.

We have known compromise in our lives. We are soiled. The people to whom I preach are probably very similar to the readers of this book. We gather on Sunday mornings as a collection of liars, adulterers, cheats, fakers, gossips, drunks, idolaters, doubters – sinners every one of us, not least of whom is the pastor. But we gather in the hope that we can, as a result of Jesus' call, stop nodding over coffee and blindly following the breakneck pace of life in the world. Jesus has said to each one, "I know who you are, and I want you to follow me." So we gather because we have taken the first halting little baby steps to get up from our tax booth and go after the Prince of Peace and the Lord of Love. With a similar hope, perhaps, you are persisting through these pages.

Jesus comes to us even when we are years down the wrong road. Though we feel isolated by our compromises, his voice reaches the innermost depths with an invitation to return to fellowship. Jesus finds and warms the long-buried heart, even when we thought it was lost and turned to stone. His invitation searches out the child who still yearns to be picked up and held close. We thought we had put too many years of determined self-reliance between us and our need for him. But he breaks through. When we have decided that we have simply done too much wrong to ever be worthy again, he calls us to himself. The sheer pace of life and the demands of routine may have us locked into a course, but he can make a new road. With those two words, "Follow me," everything can change.

———— ◆ ————

*D*o you yet regard us, dear Jesus? We are so far down roads we never meant to take. We have thought you could never find us. We have feared there is no way back home. But for all the hardness of our exterior, all the face we have put over our choices, we are soft and needy inside. Call us forth and we will come to you. See more in us than we see in ourselves, and we will leap to follow you. We long for the new life you bring. Amen.

CHAPTER FOUR

Not Distracted by Externals
Luke 7:1-10

> *So Jesus went with them.*
>
> Luke 7:6

Jesus never seemed moved by the worldly position of those around him. He was not put off by the scandalous occupation of Levi, the tax collector. Nor was he overly impressed when he appeared before the Roman governor, Pilate. Even his enemies admitted, "Teacher, we know you are a man of integrity. You aren't swayed by men, because you pay no attention to who they are; but you teach the way of God in accordance with the truth" (Mark 12:14). Jesus would not perform signs or miracles for those who demanded proof of his authority. He could walk safely past those who wanted to seize him. And he infuriated those who pressed him by ever turning the tables on all their theological traps. Jesus could not be had by any kind of force.

Yet, one could get his attention simply by asking. He seems to have been delighted when people would invite his presence. The crowds hungry for bread, longing for healing, or eager for teaching from God moved Jesus to respond compassionately. Knowing the fickleness of the human heart, Jesus seemed to treasure the moments of honest faith from ordinary people. Perhaps because he understood so keenly how the crowds would one day reject him, he prized every instance of an open, welcoming heart. Jesus could not be coerced by any kind of power, but he could be deeply moved by those who sought him honestly.

We see Jesus' discernment of motivations in the story of the Roman centurion found in Luke 7. An appeal was made to Jesus based on the external worthiness of this particular man. And Jesus respond favorably to the request. Yet, as the story unfolds, we see that Jesus had not been influenced by the way others had praised the military officer. Something else moved him. Perhaps if we can understand Jesus' loving regard for this centurion, then we may find a clue as to how we may receive this Lord who comes to us in every hour.

A centurion's servant

The occupying government of Rome left soldiers in every conquered region. A centurion was a commander in charge of a company of one hundred soldiers. Though the different centurions in a Roman legion might vary in rank and responsibility, all enjoyed a good measure of prestige. They were well paid, and it appears that Rome encouraged stability so that a centurion, though not native, might spend many years among a particular people. Interestingly, these mid-level officers are most often described favorably in the New Testament. In contrast to most of the Pharisees and scribes of Israel, several centurions exhibit great faith. Cornelius is described in Acts as a man of prayer and generosity to the poor, and it was a centurion who cried out at the death of Jesus, "Surely he was the Son of God!" (Matt. 27:54).

As Jesus entered the village of Capernaum again, Luke tells us that the local centurion's servant was gravely ill. The Roman officer was concerned about his treasured servant. Having heard of Jesus' effectiveness as a healer, the centurion wanted Jesus to come. He could have sent a detachment of soldiers to bring Jesus to him. But the centurion wanted to persuade Jesus to come voluntarily. So he sent some of the Jewish elders to Jesus. This seems a sound strategy. The centurion was a Gentile from an occupying government. Jesus was a religious teacher of

Israel. What could be more effective than to send some of his peers, some fellow spiritual leaders, who might know how to catch his ear and convince him to move the centurion to the top of his list?

The elders were only too happy to go, for it gave them a chance to return a favor. This centurion was an ally. Luke tells us that they "pleaded earnestly" with Jesus, "This man deserves to have you do this, because he loves our nation and has built our synagogue" (Luke 7:4-5). The elders appealed to all the ways the centurion was worthy. He was a big giver. It is possible that this officer had paid for construction of the very synagogue where Jesus had taught. And, the elders insisted, the centurion was much more than a Roman. He loved the land and the people under his guard. As a pastor, I can understand the appeal. I would surely rearrange my schedule if some of our church officers came to tell me that I could do something significant for a man who not only loved our church but had made possible the very building in which I am writing these words!

And Jesus, without saying any words that were recorded, went with them. Was it possible that he was persuaded by such worldly motivations as I am? The text doesn't tell us at first. He simply started on his way.

But say the word

But then they were interrupted. The centurion had sent a group of his friends with a message. "Lord, don't trouble yourself, for I do not deserve to have you come under my roof. That is why I did not even consider myself worthy to come to you. But say the word, and my servant will be healed. For I myself am a man under authority, with soldiers under me. I tell this one 'Go,' and he goes; and that one, 'Come,' and he comes. I say to my servant, 'Do this,' and he does it" (Luke 7:6-8).

The centurion had not come to Jesus personally. It was not arrogance, however, that motivated him to send others on his behalf, but humility. He did not want to come and bear down on Jesus with the authority his uniform and very presence would imply. The centurion did not feel worthy. And further consideration made him even more reluctant. Familiar with Jewish customs, the officer would have known that had Jesus entered his house, the home of a Gentile, he would have become ritually unclean. Jesus would then have had to undergo the imposition of ceremonial cleansing. The centurion realized that such a burden was not necessary for Jesus. All Jesus had to do was say the word. This soldier who had sworn loyalty to the emperor of Rome recognized in Jesus an authority that extended not just over mere nations, but over the very powers and forces of life and death, illness and healing, body and soul.

Jesus was amazed at such understanding. "I tell you," he said, "I have not found such great faith even in Israel" (Luke 7:9). What moved Jesus was neither the good works nor the worldly power of this centurion, but his extraordinary faith. Jesus, who always saw past external claims to worthiness, was deeply pleased that the Roman officer also saw below the surface to the heart of the matter. The centurion, from a distance and without ever coming face to face with him, recognized the truth of who had come to Israel. It almost goes without saying that when the messengers returned home, they found the servant healed.

Such a story can relieve us and frighten us at the same time. The chilling part is that all the worldly connections and credentials we try to build have no power to motivate Jesus to come to us. We may have learned how to avoid lines, how to get in to see busy, prestigious officials who are too busy for most, how to keep the auto mechanic from cheating us and even how to get a carpenter to come to our house on time. But none of our skills will help us with Jesus. He is not moved by our externals. What we have spent so much time learning and becoming does not help us with the Lord who has authority over life and death.

The relief, therefore, is that we do not have to maintain the facades that keep us going in the world. Jesus wants something from much closer to our hearts. Our external activities, however, may provide the tap which will drive down into the faith of a receptive soul. By carefully considering the way the centurion spoke to Jesus, we may uncover a pattern that can be employed in our reception of Christ.

The pattern of faithful welcome

First, the centurion dismissed all talk of his supposed deserving. In the message he sent to Jesus, he was saying in effect, "Others declare that I am worthy to have you do this for me because I am a friend of Israel. They praise me for being devout and giving a lot of money to the synagogue. But you and I know better. I know my sin. I know that nothing I do can establish my worthiness before one such as you. Do not trouble yourself on my behalf. Do not soil yourself by coming into the house of a Gentile. I am not as worthy as they say."

Second, the centurion's frank assessment of his worth did not, however, stop him from appealing to Jesus. He still had a need and he knew Jesus could meet it. So he redirected his appeal. The centurion continued his message by drawing from his own life experience of how things get done. He expressed his knowledge of how authority works: "I say 'Do this,' and it is done. I know how power is exercised in the world. People in command issue orders and those under their authority enact those instructions. I know this both from obeying and giving orders."

Third, he made a link of faith between his understanding of the world and the person of Jesus. As he asked Jesus to just say the word, the centurion was implying, "If I have authority like this in the world, surely you have even more authority. If one such as I can command soldiers, then one such as you can speak in the realm of nature and the powers which influence health will obey you. My servant can be healed if you but give the word."

By understanding his own life, and then looking away from himself to Jesus, the centurion understood something of Jesus that others had missed. The centurion had analyzed his place, but he did not remain self-absorbed. He looked beyond himself to Christ, employing his knowledge of his own occupation to assist his understanding of who Jesus was and how he worked in the world. In other words, he allowed his subjective experience of life to increase his objective knowledge of the Son of God. The centurion compared his life to Jesus, and used the lens of his occupation to magnify his faith in the Christ who had come among us. And so a dynamic connection was made.

As we seek to receive Jesus wholeheartedly so that he fills and transforms more and more of our lives, the centurion's message can be a guide for us. We may apply this pattern to our own prayers. And then, perhaps, a deeper interaction will occur. Let us consider this form from the point of view of an accountant, a mother, and a lawyer.

Three examples

A man who is an accountant might begin his prayers identifying his occupation and what he has noted about it: "O Lord, I work with numbers. I am concerned with order and balances. I strive to keep my client's books accurate and useful. Under my guidance, strengths can be maximized and weaknesses reduced. When others are confused by the figures, I can make sense of them. My work requires that I find things that are lost and bring to light what is hidden. Based on the numbers, I can chart the future and make recommendations for the best course forward."

And then he might admit how others' estimation of his worth might raise his expectations in knowing God: "Jesus, I know that people have relied on my honesty for years. They count on my integrity and the plain sense I make of things. People might expect that if anyone should have an honest relationship with you, it would be me."

But the faithful accountant would go on, like the centurion, to dismiss his external success as any reason for Jesus' attention: "But Lord, you and I know better. It's not just the mistakes I have made in business. I hide the facts from you. I can't make the books of my life balance, nor my accounts with you square up. I'd never survive a spiritual audit."

And then he could make the connection of faith, based on the worth of Jesus, but seen through the lens of his occupation: "Nevertheless, dear Jesus, I know that you bring order and balance to the whole universe. You can do that in my life. You can devise the plan which will shore up my weaknesses while I am serving from my strengths. You can bring to light even the facts and figures I have tried to bury, and from that truth, you can make me free and whole. You are the great Accountant whose justice is love, whose accuracy is grace. Come in and settle my accounts."

Or a mother might pray on behalf of a child, naming her concern and why others would deem her worthy of an answered prayer: "O Lord, I am worried about my son, who seems no longer to know up from down, right from wrong. He is hurting himself and I don't know what to do. Others tell me that if you hear anyone's prayers, you should hear mine. For I have been a devoted mother, trying always to set a good example. I have cared all these years so deeply for my children."

This mother would not be fooled by such praise, but would go on to use her experience to make a connection with Christ: "But Lord, do not trouble yourself because of my presumed worthiness. You know the selfish ambitions I have had for this boy. You know the ways I have tried to make him in my image. You know the pride I felt when I compared him to others. No, I am not worthy to have you under the roof of my well-praised house. Still, I care for him. As a mother, I have spent sleepless nights in prayer and worry for my son. I have tried to do all I can. I have wanted so much for him. And I know, that even more than I, you love him, too. As I have watched him, even more faithfully, you have kept watch. O dear Father, out of your motherly concern, pour your healing power upon my boy. Tend him now as I long to do. Speak your love to him. Only say the word and it will be done. Only embrace him in your arms and he will come home to you."

Next, a respected attorney might offer prayers on behalf of a loved one. She lifts up why others might deem her worthy so that such externals can be cleared away: "O Lord, I am praying for healing. I am asking that you who came into the world would come powerfully into the life of my loved one. People say I am deserving of your attention because I am respected as a defender of the poor. I champion the hurt and neglected. But you know my heart. You know every vicious thrill of victory and every contemptuous thought I have had for adversaries and clients alike. Were it my worthiness that counted, I would have to urge you not to trouble yourself. But you alone are the worthy one."

Then she uses her occupation to focus her prayers and to illuminate the characteristics of Jesus: "As I have learned no longer to be surprised by any human behavior, so you know us through and through and yet do not turn away. I have helped people work through ridiculous messes and horrible abuses, but even more, O Lord, you are the friend of the friendless. You are the great Advocate. You specialize in making glorious new lives out of the ashes of the old. I have learned how to use words to persuade on behalf of others, but you utter words on our behalf at the right hand of the Father. Your prayers are the true and effective words of life. So out of that advocacy, out of such prayers, you have the power to influence this situation. You can make sense of this illness for us. You can plead my loved one's case and create healing. Only say the word and it will be so."

Making the connection

Whatever we do in the world, there is something in it that partakes of the nature and love of God. Whether it's simply expending energy to dress yourself so another doesn't have to or performing arthroscopic surgery to enable another to walk, whether you clean the house or guide a corporation, you exercise skill and power that has its source in God. That means there is a point of connection between us and Jesus that can deepen our reception of him. When we name the quality in our activities that is also in Jesus Christ though in a higher, purer way, then we align our lives with the will and character of God.

Jesus comes to us undaunted by any of our external trappings. He was always pleased to be invited into another's home, another's life, even if going under the roof of such a house would appear to make him unclean. The good news in the story of the centurion and his servant is stated so simply by Luke, "Jesus went with them" (Luke 7:6). The even more tremendous news is that he didn't go because the centurion was a man of authority, wealth, loyalty or generosity. Jesus comes in response to the humblest invitation and cannot be influenced by any worldly art of persuasion.

As he's making his way toward the home of our lives, however, there is something we may do to welcome him heartily. We may consider him carefully. Based on what we know of life, we tell him not why we're worthy, but why he's worthy. We allow our experience to be a lens through which we look away from ourselves to him. We gaze upon him, and the lens of what we know focuses and intensifies our praise. Such prayers Jesus called faith, and with the message of the centurion, he was most pleased.

Gracious Jesus, others have called us worthy of your attention, but we both know better. We are not worthy in ourselves to have you come into the house of our lives. Yet we know that you are the one who comes to us in every hour. You are the one who invites us to come to you. You are the one who asks to come within our hearts. So based on your worthiness and not our own, we say Yes. Come in dear Lord. Bring to us your righteousness, your healing and wholling power. At your word, we will be transformed. Amen.

CHAPTER FIVE

In the Midst of Loss

Luke 7:11-17

When the Lord saw her, his heart went out to her.

Luke 7:13

I received an e-mail recently from a professor who has become a friend as well as a mentor. He answered a theological question and shared his progress on his work. But he also made the effort to encourage me in *my* work. He made sure to express his love and prayers not only for me but for my family. Any way we could see more of each other would please him as he offered to help me with a project for a graduate degree. Moreover, he invited my prayers as his wife faced the imminent loss of her sister. I felt let into his heart. The entire message buoyed my spirits for days.

I wondered why he took such an interest in me. We really hadn't known each other that long nor worked together very closely. He didn't need anything from me and so there was no gain to be had by flattering me unnecessarily. And there is nothing particular to set me apart from other students or colleagues. Then I realized that I had put my finger on it. This dear man has a wide open heart, bathed in years of prayer, and turned out toward others. No special merit is required to receive it. He exhibits that rare, wonderful quality of spiritual maturity. Love overflows from the center of someone who has spent decades learning to love and to know the God who is love. And it draws people. I want to be in the company of a person who loves so genuinely.

Jesus revealed such a heart as he walked among us. He spent hours in prayer with his Father. The result of such times of withdrawal from others was not self-absorption but a watchful concern for the situations of those he encountered. His deep connection to the Father inspired his overflowing compassion for those he met. It is no wonder great crowds followed him. Such love is compelling. We are nourished by its life-giving warmth.

After Jesus had healed the centurion's servant in Capernaum, he made his way to a small mountain village called Nain. As he approached the town gate, he ran into a funeral procession. In an open coffin, the body of a deceased young man was being borne to a tomb in the rock of the mountainside. His mother led the way. Luke makes sure we understand the situation: the dead man was "the only son of his mother, and she was a widow" (Luke 7:12). In other words, the woman had no one to look after her now. She had already been bereaved once before. Now there was no hope of the family name being continued. Her means of support and protection were gone.

Jesus' keen eye for others would have helped him assess the situation quickly. He understood that before him was the tragedy of mortal frailty. Here was inconsolable loss. The townspeople had rallied around this woman now, but a dark future lay before her.

His heart went out

Then, so simply and elegantly, Luke tells us how this scene affected Jesus. "When the Lord saw her, his heart went out to her ..." (Luke 7:13). Looking upon her condition, Jesus was moved. He saw her; he did not avert his gaze or hurry by about other business. He looked at her until her pain became his pain. Of all the things we consider about Jesus in this book, this one is of supreme importance: The Son of God came among us in order to behold the true situation of life in this world. In Jesus, God looked upon us from the point of view of a man. From within our human condition he felt the terrible way our lives and loves slip through our fingers like sand. He knows how it is with us. He *knows*, from the inside out. Jesus knows.

And what he saw moved Jesus in the very center of his being. The Greek word Luke uses is so rich with meaning that it can scarcely be translated in a simple phrase. It derives from a noun that referred to the "inward parts" of a sacrifice, such as the heart and kidneys. That word later came to mean the "portion of our inward parts as the seat of feelings" and the "center of human feeling and sensibility generally."[1] When Jesus saw the widow on the way to bury her only son, he was moved in that innermost place of body and soul. It was that deeply affected heart of Jesus which went out to her. Seeing a woman who was grieved and wounded in her depths moved Jesus in his own depths. Then, the compassion of his heart, wounded in sympathy, reached out to come alongside the broken heart of this widow. To render the Greek with but one word, we could say that Jesus *heart-reached* toward her.

Interestingly, the use of this Greek word is reserved in the Gospels for the feelings of Jesus alone, or for those characters he himself used in parables to represent the loving mercy of God. This is the same word employed when Matthew tells us "When he saw the crowds, he *had compassion* on them, because they were harassed and helpless, like sheep without a shepherd (Matt. 9:36). Jesus used it when he described the *mercy* the Good Samaritan both felt and enacted when he saw the man who had been beaten along the Jericho Road. And this *heart-reaching* describes why the father in Jesus' parable hitched up his robes and ran to embrace his prodigal son when he saw him returning down the road at last. Love that arises from seeing the condition of another is a God-like quality. Our Lord looked upon those he encountered so openly that he allowed himself to be moved in his very depths. His innermost being is pure love, so when he was moved, he *heart-reached*, overflowing in words and acts of tender compassion.

Giving back what was lost

Then Jesus spoke to the widow of Nain, "Don't cry" (Luke

7:13). We may use the same words to comfort someone. Often, though, all we can offer is our loving presence. We can't do much to stop the cause of the tears. But Jesus urged the woman not to weep because he could restore the life of her son. Luke tells us that Jesus touched the coffin, stopping the procession. This was even more a breach of etiquette then than it would be now. Touching a dead body or its coffin made one ritually unclean, much as entering the Gentile centurion's house would have defiled Jesus. An elaborate cleansing ritual would need to be followed. This uncleanness did not deter Jesus. He put his hand on the coffin and spoke, "Young man, I say to you, get up!" (Luke 7:14). Immediately the man sat up and began speaking. Indeed, there was no more need of tears unless they were tears of joy.

The next line in Luke's telling of the story might be easily overlooked. But it reveals still more depth in Jesus' love. We read, "Jesus gave him back to his mother" (Luke 7:15). Jesus had retrieved from death the life that was lost. Now he closed the loop by giving the young man back to his mother. He restored her son to her. So often we hear people say, "God took my husband home last year," or "It was time for God to take her." I'm not sure if this "taking" is theologically the most accurate way to describe God's part in death. But it surely does *feel* like our loved ones are taken away from us. Here we see clearly Jesus' compassionate response to such loss: he gives back what seemed irrevocably gone.

As we might expect, the crowd who witnessed this miracle was filled with awe. They praised God. They began to take hope in their situation. "God has come to help his people," (Luke 7:16) they began to say. He hadn't forgotten them or their suffering. Rather, God came to be with them, and he came to be with us even now.

This story of the only son restored to his widowed mother tells how Jesus desires us to be with one another. The Triune God who has his being in relationship created *us* for loving relationship. We entered the world already relating to our parents and siblings, and many of us have since been granted spouses, friends and children of our own. Even as God enjoys the ever-flowing communion between the Father, Son and Spirit, he intends these relationships of ours to be flourishing and life-giving as well. Of course sin twists our love; accidents in a fallen world tear us apart too soon; illness and mortality steal us away from each other. We are frail. We do not mirror the life of God as we were meant. But God intends to restore life, not just in the abstract, but in loving relationships. He wants to give us back to each other!

I believe that God still has the power to raise the dead. I also believe that such power is only rarely exercised in the present condition of the world (and never in my experience). Rather, the times Jesus raised others from the dead were a sign and foretaste to us of what is to come. Jesus' resurrection has shattered the powers of sin and death. He has opened the way to eternal life. The New Testament understanding of this everlasting life is the resurrection of the body at the last trumpet. We will live with God in spiritual, incorruptible bodies.

To me, this passage from Luke implies that we will live in relationship to one another as well. We will know each other, and our communion then will make even the best of relationships now seem as but a shadow. Jesus gave the young man back to his mother. The one who looks upon us with such *heart-reaching* yearns to restore our relationships to life and health. He promises a day when "God himself will be with them and be their God. He will wipe every tear from their eyes. There will be no more death or mourning or crying or pain, for the old order of things" will have passed into a new heavens and a new earth (Rev. 21:3-4).

The hope today

But where does that leave us in the present moment? How is such life-restoring compassion available to us this side of heaven? Jesus said in the Gospel of John, "Your forefathers ate the manna in the desert, yet they died" (John 6:49). Even those who had been spectacularly led by God through the parted waters of the Red Sea, and then were fed miraculously in the wilderness by the daily gift of the dew-like bread called manna, still suffered the curse of mortality. Though God acts powerfully in our lives and some of us have even seen wondrous healings, yet ultimately we all must give way to death. Jesus knew that the people he healed or raised from the dead would still perish, and he added, "But here is the bread that comes down from heaven which a man may eat and not die. I am the living bread that came down from heaven. If anyone eats of this bread, he will live forever ... Whoever eats my flesh and drinks my blood has eternal life and I will raise him up at the last day" (John 6:50-51, 54). There is the promise here of life to come through union with Christ. But notice the present tense "has eternal life." Something about being in relationship to Jesus gives us his everlasting life in present experience. We have his quickening love right now. Before ever we realize the final victory of the resurrection, we may drink deeply of Jesus' life-giving love.

Jesus still beholds us with eyes that see and a heart that reaches forth. For example, Jesus sees the widow and our Lord, who was known as "the man acquainted with grief" (Isa. 53:3), understands her loneliness. Amidst tearful prayers she feels him come alongside her. He whispers in the night, "You will see him again. Because I live, you also will live (John 14:19). Death is not the end. Wait. There is more." Beyond hope, she knows then that Jesus understands, and she believes his words.

And Jesus sees the man who has lost the second of his parents in the last year. This fellow realizes that there is now no one in the generation above him. There are no elders to turn to; he's it. And he feels alone. But seeing him, Jesus' heart goes out to him even now. The peace that passes understanding is gently offered. And because Jesus, as bone of our bone and flesh of our flesh, experienced himself separation from his Father on the cross, the peace he offers this man is real.

Meanwhile, the tired caregiver going daily to pour life into a lost cause is not unnoticed by our Christ. Jesus feels along with him the sharp paradox in tending this steady decline in a loved one. Death would be a welcome relief from suffering, but oh such a loss to the one who has rearranged all his life around the care! Jesus sees, he feels, and he speaks to the heart, "Don't cry; I'm here. Never will I leave you; never will I forsake you (Heb. 13:5). I am able to keep you even through this tension, even through this exhaustion."

And this very moment, Jesus sees the woman who is single again, and watches her face as the coffin carrying her expectations of what life was supposed to be like passes by. He sees the crowd surrounding her with support for the moment, but his heart goes out to her as he considers her coming midnights alone. "This is not the end of love in your life. I have plans for you other than despair," he says. "Will you take my yoke upon you, and learn from me? Trust me. I will lead you to the other side of this rending."

Elsewhere, there are children caught in the crossfire of their parents' anger, and Christ feels their bewilderment; he knows their fear and he's not surprised at their anger. Jesus' heart goes out to them. He yearns toward them even now. He calls to the child who has run to a loud, broken, dangerous place, trying desperately to be as lost as she feels. And he says, "My sheep know my voice. And I call them by name. No one can snatch them out of my hand (John 10:27-28). Will you let me find you? When your home is crazy and unsafe will you come home to me?" God truly has come to help his people. He has sent his Son, and Christ continues to come to us in every hour.

But will he raise the dead? Will he heal an eighty-year old of illness and provide a fountain of youth? Will he make a marriage work again with a snap of his fingers? Will he remove the sharpness of loss in middle age? Or eliminate the long road to self-worth and self-love for the damaged child? Though such instant miracles are possible, they are not likely. They do not seem to be the usual manner of Christ's work among us in this life.

More than sympathy

Still today, though, Jesus can touch coffins and stop funeral processions. And his coming is more than personal comfort in troubled times, as wonderful as that is. He brings power to transform. To take just one example, Jesus can stop the funeral procession that is carrying our youth out of town to the tombs. There are too many that are lying in a coffin made of the lies that thrilling, vivid experiences or more new possessions will satisfy the restless soul. There are too many seeking the love they crave by giving up their bodies to any who will have them, and they're heading for the tombs. There are too many who are drinking and drugging to escape the deathliness of their lives unaware that the coffin is rolling quickly. Jesus looks upon their confusion, feels their stress, hears their anger and understands the pressure they're under. He can fill the vacant places in their hearts. He can offer another way. He waits, I believe, for his people, the church, to give voice to his heart, and speak in his name "Young man, I say 'Get up!' Young woman, 'Arise!'"

Jesus can give the youth back to their parents. And his power can return the busy, distracted, confused parents back to their children again. At his word, the funeral procession of our culture can be halted. He can interrupt our march to the tombs. By Jesus' word, before it is too late, we can realize the dead end of our ambitions and the deathly pace with which we pursue entertainment. There can again be time for one another and a mutual interest that melts away the anger. Relationships can be healed by the loving power of Christ.

He still beholds the world for which he died. He looks until his heart breaks with grief, and then he pours out his compassion. And there is quickening power in that love. But it seems that he waits for his body to enact the desires of his heart. His body is us, the Church, and the world in the grief of its endless procession to the tombs waits for Christ's arms to hold, for his mouth to speak comfort, and for his hands to touch with new life. The Christ who came to the widow of Nain comes to us still. And he sends us still, right to the hopeless places with the hope of Christ. When we begin to act with his beholding, *heart-reaching* compassion, the world will be drawn to hear of our Lord. Such love is simply irresistible, for it leads people to the very heart of God.

L ook upon our living and our dying, dear
Jesus. Allow your sight to penetrate your
heart and then reach toward us. For we are in
need of your care. See our plight and do not hold
yourself far from us. Touch even the coffins and
bring new life where there is none. Your love,
shining forth from your great heart, is our desire.
Amen.

Endnote

1. Helmut Köster, *splanchnon*, in *Theological Dictionary of the
   New Testament*, vol. vii (Grand Rapids: Eerdmans, 1971), pp.
   548-555.

CHAPTER SIX

When We Are Being Torn Apart

Luke 8:26-39

When they came to Jesus, they found the man ...
sitting at Jesus' feet, dressed and in his right mind.

Luke 8:35

Our family lives in a small city in North Carolina. Our house is actually several miles from the town center, so it's rural enough that we don't tap into city sewer lines. Recently we had to have our septic tank drainage lines rebuilt, and each stage of the process was the cause of no small amount of anxiety for me. A huge backhoe came to dig up our yard. For several precarious hours, sewage was exposed. What if rain came and work had to be stopped? Or what if the men took a break and then went to another job while the lines were still open? Next, several large trucks filled with tons of gravel growled up our quiet street. Would they crack the driveway or break our beloved trees? Would they arouse suspicions in our neighbors? And then, when they were finished, I worried if the yard would be level, if the grass would return soon or whether the dirt would wash down next door.

Thankfully, none of these nightmares came to pass. I don't like thinking about waste, and I particularly don't like uncovering it. Even worse, I don't want to be at risk for my neighbors to encounter in any way my sewage. But this, I realized on that anxious day, is a metaphor. We want what stinks to be safely carried away. We don't want anyone to even think about what's going on under the surface of lovingly tended lives. But from time to time the waste disposal system ages or simply fails. Then, we face either a massive, disgusting breakdown or an all too public noisy, messy repair job. Either way, anyone can see we have a problem. Life is getting torn open.

As a pastor, I've had to go a lot of places I didn't want to go. There are nursing homes – not of the wealthy who can pay to be tended but of the poor – which reek of decaying life that can no longer maintain itself. Ravaged bodies litter the hallways. Occasionally a hand will reach out to stop me in my quick walk to the room I must visit. My heart breaks but my body recoils. What can I do? There are the homes of alcoholics whose cover on their addiction has been, like my septic system, falling apart. The air is thick with tension as family members walk near the edge of confronting the problem, but are terrified of the abyss below. There is the homeless shelter where I spent a terrified night listening to the boom of radios in passing cars mingle with the snores of men who've walked in valleys of a darkness my eyes cannot penetrate. There is the room where a man packed to leave as we begged him not to walk out on his precious family.

I've never had the courage to stay very long in these places where life is blowing open. They frighten me. And I just don't know what I'm supposed to do for the people there. Others, I know, have been called to live in these wastelands. They make their homes in the broken places, and God sustains them, and they do ministry at a profound level. I prefer to retreat to my safe home (drainage field problems notwithstanding!) where I can pretend that life will not fall apart and all my loved ones will always be safe. Thankfully, Jesus was not afraid to enter the blast zones of human existence. Nor was he reluctant to engage those whom he encountered there. Jesus walked into chaos and stilled the storms. He willingly faced the rending forces and brought his wholeness to them.

Legion: A reality beyond usual sight

With the story of the man once called Legion, we step into suddenly deep waters. We have an account of Jesus healing someone bound by destructive, evil powers. This account of Legion immediately raises the whole issue of the reality of a spiritual realm that intersects with this earthly, daily world of ours. The contemporary worldview is challenged. Culturally, we tend to think that all of reality is physical. What is can be described and contained within the material world. If it can't be quantified, analyzed, tested and verified by our methods, then it is not real. But the biblical world view allows for the presence in the world of spiritual forces greater than we. And some of them are hostile to the well-being of humanity. These powers are larger than any one individual though they act to influence and damage individual lives. Some of our woes, then, are caused and sustained by these supra-personal, malevolent powers.

Before us is the reality of evil. There is more destruction in the world than the sum of individual behaviors can account. A continuing struggle exists between the creative, healing power of God's love and the disintegrating, debilitating power of evil. One glance at any day's newspaper provides sufficient description for those who will see. Even though a secular media will not generally acknowledge the potency of the spiritual realm, its reports provide a constant stream of evidence for it. Whether we recognize it or not, we are each part of this struggle, and each responsible for a portion of it.

Jesus and his disciples had just come through a fierce storm on the Sea of Galilee. They landed on the outskirts of the region of the Gerasenes, and were immediately met by a man from the city, who now lived out among the tombs. The man was naked and bloody. Chain links hung loosely from the manacles that cut into his wrists. Myriad expressions competed for time on the stage of his tired, dirty face. Conflicting emotions ran through him constantly, but especially now as he was provoked by the presence of Jesus.

The man ran up to Jesus and fell down before him as if to worship. But the first words out of his mouth were hardly reverent. He shouted, shrill and hoarse, "What do you want with me, Jesus, Son of the Most High God? I beg you, don't torture me!" (Luke 8:28). The very nearness of Jesus was sweet torment. He couldn't stay away; he couldn't stand to be near him. He called Jesus the Son of God, demonstrating more recognition than the religious officials, yet he expected to be punished. The text tells us that Jesus had been commanding an evil spirit to come out of the man. It was agony to him.

"What is your name?" Jesus asked.

"Legion," he replied, "because many demons had gone into him" (Luke 8:30). And the demons begged Jesus not to command them to go into the Abyss. They did not want to be disembodied. They pleaded to be sent into a nearby herd of pigs. And Jesus granted their request. Immediately, the swine went mad and rushed off the slope into the sea where they drowned.

The swineherds saw that their pigs had been destroyed and ran to raise the alarm in town. When the people rushed out to find Jesus, they saw the man who had been known as Legion "sitting at Jesus' feet, dressed and in his right mind" (Luke 8:35). The people were gripped with fear and begged Jesus to leave. So he started for his boat. The healed man asked Jesus if he could go with him. But the Lord refused, saying, "Return home and tell how much God has done for you" (Luke 8:39).

In the grip of the powers

The man known as Legion had lived among the tombs. At that time, the Gerasene dead were buried in caves in the craggy hills. Legion lived out there, away from normal society. According to Mark's account of this event, he cried out continually, gashing himself with sharp stones (Mark 5:5). He inflicted pain upon himself. For he was caught in the grip of powers he could not control. The people could do little for him. All attempts to bind him ended with Legion bursting asunder the chains and screaming away to the hills. Legion could not control himself; he could not stop the self-inflicted damage.

Is this story too fantastic to be anything like us? So it may seem until we consider:

Perhaps once you swore, for the thousandth time, that you would be more patient with your family. You woke up with a fresh start and went to the breakfast table with hope. But every little thing you saw made you furious. You began to criticize everyone, despite your resolutions. You shouted over things that didn't matter. The children were in tears. Your spouse was disgusted. Breakfast was ruined. And you were a sweaty mess, alone, dwelling among the tombs, wondering why you had no control over the rage within you.

Or perhaps once again you watched yourself sabotage the possibility for love. Whenever someone wanted to take you out of the desert and back into the city, you fell apart. You remembered the past and could not get over it. Joy, love, friendship, life beckoned but you, out of a pattern as old as your childhood, preferred to live among the tombs. You wanted to be where the dead things are, where the memories still walk around in the twilight, where the stones are sharp and can be used to punish you for your mistakes. Every time someone offered kindness, the possibility for relationship, something beyond your control shrieked within you. You broke away from the arms that wanted to hold you against the dark. You ran for the tombs, back to your habitual depression. There you gash yourself and long to join the dead ones in their graves.

Or maybe it was the time you realized you were addicted to work. That was the first Saturday in weeks that you hadn't brought work home or gone back to the office. You had sworn to yourself that you would take time to enjoy the home you labored to have, to pay attention to the children who were growing up a year every time you turned around, to notice your spouse and remember why you got married. But as your son kicked at the ball, you were thinking about the call you had to make on Monday. While your daughter told you a story, you strategized about a meeting. You looked at your wife, but saw past her to the difficult employee at the office. As hard as you tried, you could not make yourself feel present and happy in your home. You no longer knew your family, and even worse, you hardly cared. For you no longer lived in a house. You dwelt among the tombs of your compulsion, and that seemed normal. By three o'clock on Saturday, you were back at the office.

There are powers which bind us and drive us. Beyond our control, they keep us from living in wholesome, healthy ways. They cause illness and create conditions under which the body cannot prosper but must, eventually, fall to disease. They get a foothold early on by the terrible things that are done to us, by our families or by the community. They grow in power when we unknowingly develop further destructive habits of our own, perhaps in compensation for pain. They flourish when we willingly continue to live out of anger, fear, bitterness, or worry. And we may have no idea how to break the cycle.

Such powers destroy not only families but whole communities. They savage churches and businesses. They prey on the weak and defenseless. Now I've never seen an evil power dressed in a red devil's suit. And the instances of graphic distortion one sees in movies are rare (yet documented). But the powers are real and prevalent. Call them demons or autonomous psychological complexes. Unmask the evil one by naming him directly or use the language of the social sciences. The fact is, people are afflicted, and there is more afoot than individual behavior or sin can account for. As Paul wrote, we are in a struggle "not against flesh and blood," but "against the powers of this dark world" (Eph. 6:12). Evil is real and it makes us sick. It tears us apart. We need the power of Christ Jesus the Lord of all to heal us.

To be clothed and in a right mind

Our story says that after Jesus cast the demons from him, the man who had been Legion sat down at Jesus' feet, dressed and in his right mind. How great a premium do we place on this kind of healing? What is it worth to be clothed and in your right mind? Perhaps the idea of evil still seems too fantastic and this picture of healing seems too trivial. Unless ...

Unless you wake up on the floor of the living room with a broken bottle next to your face. You wonder, "Who put the kids to bed? What time is it? How did I get here?" What would it be worth in that moment to be healed: clothed, and in your right mind?

Unless the mantle of the family's worries has always fallen to you. They run off into the world, never giving a second thought to what they are doing or what harm could come. You are worrying enough for all of them. You wake constantly during the night. You try to pray but anxiety prevents you. You don't know how to give it to God. You are losing weight, or gaining too much. You're a bundle of fear and you can't stop the horrors of your imagination. How much is it worth then to have the hold of the powers broken so you can be clothed and in your right mind?

Unless chronic ill health keeps you from any semblance of a normal life. You are disgusted at being so dependent on others. You are tired, so tired of the pain. You don't know why you can't get better. Prayer is difficult; getting outside of yourself even harder. You just feel good for nothing like this. How would it be to be sitting at the feet of Jesus, clothed in something besides pajamas, with your mind and health restored?

Unless you have been pummeled by people who inflict their personal rage and suffering on you. They whittle down your esteem with their snipes. They mash down your sense of self with a barrage of demands, criticisms, and dismissals. Your health begins to give way. And then, like sharks smelling blood, all kinds of people begin to take bites out of you. Everyone wants to take a shot, take advantage, get a piece. Your life is out of control. When you are being bounced and whacked like a tennis ball, and the game is not your own, what would it be worth then to have the accusations stilled, the demands silenced, to be sitting clothed and quiet at the feet of Jesus?

The God who will go anywhere to find us

The story of Legion tells us that there are some illnesses which can only be cured supernaturally. Only the power of God can break the grip of the powers and set us free. We are drawn to Jesus as our hope for healing. But note that we, like Legion and the townspeople, are also terrified of him. Sometimes we get so used to the torn up way things are that we consider the situation normal. And we will then resist Jesus' demands to change. We'll have to overcome our initial reluctance at inviting the power of

Christ to make us well.

Our hope, though, is in the God who will go anywhere in order to find us and bring us home. Jesus went to the tombs where a wild man came shrieking out at him. He did not run away or flinch at the severity of the man's problem. Jesus spoke to him and broke the hold of the powers that harmed him. In his days among us, Jesus went everywhere that people were. He goes everywhere now. There is no place closed to him. There is no land of sin he will not traverse to rescue a sinner. There is no dungeon he will not brave to set a prisoner free. There is no sanitarium or asylum or sick ward he will not risk to put his hands on the ill and the suffering. Into the impossible situations: the haunts of worry and fear, the tombs of depression, the prisons of addiction, the beds of incurable disease, the houses of rage. He goes wherever we are and offers a higher power for the healing of humanity.

Jesus has fought and won victory over all the powers of darkness in whatever their form. As a great priest once said, "Since Christ is raised from the dead, there is no power he has not overcome." Jesus can heal and save.

So let us run from our tombs to him, and fall at his feet. Let us be willing to leave the old ways, though the powers will cry out in protest. Let us call upon Christ to free us, cleanse us, and forgive us. He alone can so heal us that we will soon be ready to go and tell all he has done for us.

This work, however, cannot be done alone. We need each other. People who have the spiritual maturity of long-practiced intercession for others are required if the ravages of evil in our lives are to be encountered and overcome. A strong fellowship of believers is necessary for us to sustain a new life. Vibrant worship, regular Bible study and sessions of prayer are not optional. This is dangerous stuff. If you feel torn apart by forces greater than you or bound by powers beyond your control, seek mature Christian help. Don't go it alone.[1]

But at the same time, do not fear. Jesus has come even to the broken and haunted places. He is the light which shines in the darkness, and no darkness can overcome him. Jesus is the Lord of heaven and earth and he has come to find his people wherever they may have wandered or been taken. He has come to lead us home, where we may be clothed and in our right minds, sitting at his feet.

F ather, we do not like to see how caught we are in the grip of powers beyond our control. But the evidence is all around us. There are places in our lives where we are out of control. There are times when we are helpless. We do what we hate, and we bring harm to ourselves and others. Oh, deliver us with your mighty power! Speak the word to set us free. We long to be clothed and sitting at your feet. For in your service is perfect freedom. Lord Jesus Christ, come to us in the hours when we are torn apart. Bring the commanding strength of your authority to every aspect of our lives. Amen.

Endnote

1. For more on this subject, I suggest you read *The Collapse of the Brass Heaven: Rebuilding Our Worldview to Embrace the Power of God* by Zeb Bradford Long and Douglas McMurry (Grand Rapids: Zondervan, 1996). Or contact Presbyterian-Reformed Ministries International, P.O. Box 429, Black Mountain, N.C. 28711, www.prmi.org.

CHAPTER SEVEN

Even If We Are Too Little, Too Late

Matthew 14:13-21

Jesus replied, "They do not need to go away.
You give them something to eat."
Matthew 14:16

All four gospels contain the story of Jesus' miraculous feeding of the multitude. The accounts, however, set up the story in different ways, so that we receive insight into the layers of meaning in this wonderful event. Mark's account begins with the return of the disciples from a village-to-village ministry tour. "Come with me by yourselves to a quiet place and get some rest," (Mark 6:31) Jesus told them. The emphasis is on the need of the *disciples* to get away from the crowds. Matthew, however, concentrates on *Jesus'* feelings after he learned that his cousin John the Baptist had been beheaded by King Herod.

This news seems to have had a profound effect on Jesus. The two men were cousins who had known each other all their lives. Their mothers had stayed together for three months during pregnancy, and Luke tells us that John leapt in his mother Elizabeth's womb when Mary first greeted her cousin (Luke 1:41). When Jesus began his ministry at age thirty, he went to John in the wilderness for baptism. And John recognized his cousin as "the Lamb of God, who takes away the sin of the world" (John 1:29).

John and Jesus had a kinship deeper than blood for both were marked for a unique place in God's purposes of redemption. So, Matthew records that "When Jesus heard what had happened, he withdrew by boat privately to a solitary place" (Matt. 14:13). Jesus seemed to want time away from ministry to consider the loss and to pray. Perhaps he wanted to be in a place that was as lonely as he felt.

For both the disciples' and Jesus' sake, then, the story in all the gospels begins with their heading by boat toward a remote shore on the Sea of Galilee. But the crowds of people who had been coming to Jesus for teaching and healing watched where the boat went. They hurried on foot around the lake and were there waiting for Jesus when he landed. They were so desperate for what Jesus had to give that they couldn't leave him alone. Without a thought for the morrow, they had gone out into the desert to find Jesus. He wanted to be alone but, like a flock of paparazzi, the people swarmed him.

Postponing need

How do you feel when you need to be alone and someone interrupts your solitude with a demanding need? What happens when someone finds your lonely place and violates it? I asked these questions to a study group once, and they felt the way you might expect: angry, frustrated, annoyed. But then one said, "When my daughter comes to me, with a look on her face that says she really needs me, somehow I'm not mad. I'm drawn to her. I find the desire and strength to postpone my need and to be with her." Love makes room for interruptions. Compassion arises from the beholding. When the mother, tired and needy herself, looked upon her daughter and saw her little one's need, concern was evoked within her. She reached down and found the strength to give.

Matthew's version of the story says that when Jesus saw the crowd, "he had compassion on them, and healed their sick" (Matt. 14:14). The Greek word for how Jesus felt is the same as that used in the story of the raising of the widow's son. Jesus' heart went out to them. When we are moved by the sight of

another to compassion, we *heart-reach*. Mark's version adds that
as he regarded them, Jesus realized that the people were "like
sheep without a shepherd" (Mark 6:34). He looked at them so
openly that he felt within himself the very plight of their lives.
And Jesus' stirred heart then reached out toward them. He postponed his personal time and allowed their interruption. Luke tells
us that Jesus "welcomed them and spoke to them about the kingdom of God" (Luke 9:11). Though he had wanted to be alone to
deal with his grief, the sight of the crowd evoked a great welcoming in Jesus' soul. Jesus *heart-reached* toward this rabble. And so
he touched each person who came to him and healed all the sick,
until the day grew late and the sun was setting. This is a wonderful picture of the character of God. When he came among us, he
laid aside his own needs and gave without measure.

As it grew later, Jesus' disciples, who had also been postponing their need for rest and quiet time with Jesus, began to get
concerned. They went to Jesus and said, "This is a remote place,
and it's already getting late. Send the crowds away, so they can go
to the villages and buy themselves some food" (Matt. 14:15). The
disciples realized that this was not the time or the place, nor did
they have the resources to consider feeding all those people. They
were saying in effect, "Jesus, you've had a big time healing today.
It was probably just what you needed to get your mind off of
John. But enough is enough. Send the crowd away. Get some rest
(and come be alone with us). You've done your part. Send them
home."

No one need leave him

But Jesus replied to their concern with the wonderful words,
"They do not need to go away. You give them something to eat."

They do not need to go away.

Consider this crowd. They had too little and they had stayed
too late. They had gone into the remote countryside without
thought for their food or accommodation. I can hear echoes from
childhood, "This is nobody's fault but your own, young man!"
These people were a needy rabble, overly apparent for our tastes.
They wore their broken hearts on the sleeves of their robes. No

concern for Jesus himself was even considered. It's doubtful they understood half of what Jesus said. They were probably sick because they didn't know enough to take care of themselves. These were the chronically inappropriate. Many were and always had been part of the underclass that lived for the latest mass diversion from their dreary lives.

To such as these, Jesus spoke. *They do not need to go away.* This is good news beyond hope. For if they do not need to depart, then you and I do not need to leave him either. They were the neediest of the needy, unabashedly draining Jesus with their after-hours requests. And they did not need to go away, even when it was late, and Jesus was tired, and they should have known better. So you and I do not need to go away. We need only agree that we are part of that crowd, too.

For behind the tender ministrations of Estee Lauder, underneath a new spring suit, or even with our ability to keep a low profile and be very discreet about our desires, we are embarrassingly, wildly needy. We ache for an acceptance so complete and a forgiveness so deep that we can scarcely breathe the existence of our yearning even in prayer. And Jesus looking upon us, looking deeply into us, sees all, and his response is not rejection but compassion. He declares, "You do not need to go away!"

Imagine what this means: are you conceited, greedy, lustful? You do not need to go away. Are you desperate, enraged, violent at heart? You do not need to go away. Are you unworthy, full of doubts, ignorant about the things of God? You do not need to go away. Are you a failure, are you frightened, are you broken in soul? You do not need to go away. You need only stay in the presence of Jesus and acknowledge your need. You do not need to leave him. You are already, this moment, in the presence of God. Only open yourself to your desire that Jesus regard you, touch you, and nourish you. Only come as you are and ask Jesus to mend your life and make it whole.

The wonderful exchange

The other half of Jesus' words involves our role not only as the needy crowd but as the disciples: *You give them something to eat.* Jesus asked the disciples to join in his *heart-reaching.* The disciples had no idea how this could happen. Their supply of food was only five loaves and two fish. But Jesus was undaunted. He knew their scant provisions would be more than enough to give to meet the needs of the crowd. He was confident in the resources of God and in his ability to tap that storehouse of love in whatever form was required. Jesus called for the food. "Taking the five loaves and two fish, and looking up to heaven, he gave thanks and broke the loaves. Then he gave them to the disciples, and the disciples gave them to the people. They all ate and were satisfied, and the disciples picked up twelve basketfuls of broken pieces that were left over" (Matt. 14:19-20). His disciples had indeed spread a feast in the desert.

This miraculous meal involved partaking of the very life of the Son of God who came to give himself to us. Though he was tired and grief-laden, Jesus accepted the needs of the crowd. He took what they had, the meager loaves and fish, even as he had taken what we are, meager flesh and bone. He offered what they had, even as he offered what we are, to God in thanksgiving and dedication. As he lifted his eyes to heaven, he tapped into his relationship with his Father. So the inexhaustible power of his life as Son of God flowed through the body and the hands of the Son of Man. And what insufficient food the crowd had given him was returned to them as a sumptuous feast, in which they were satisfied beyond their wildest imaginations. And still there was a bounty left over, for the meal came from the very source of creation itself.

Do you hear an echo of Holy Communion in this story? Just twelve chapters further on in his gospel, Matthew records: "While they were eating, Jesus took bread, gave thanks and broke it, and gave it to his disciples, saying, 'Take and eat, this is my body'" (Matt. 26:26). The feast in the wilderness foreshadowed the Last Supper, which itself was a sign of the complete self-giving of Jesus to us. As we shall consider more deeply in Chapter Thirteen, on the night in which he was betrayed, when Jesus was even more laden with grief and sorrow than over John's death, he *heart-reached* toward his disciples. He took up the bread and the cup, a symbol of his taking our humanity, our flesh and blood, and gave thanks. He offered himself, and us, to God. Then he offered himself in the bread and cup to the disciples. The extent of his gift would soon be seen in his death on the cross for our salvation. There, the broken body would be given for the healing of the world. The blood spilled as waste in the dirt would cause the wilderness of our need to bloom in joy (Isa. 35:1). As we partake of that holy supper, we join the needy crowd in the remote region who were not turned away but instead were fed by his own hands.

John Calvin described what occurs in the sacrament of the Lord's Supper as a *wonderful exchange*, whereby Christ takes what is ours – broken, sinful, unworthy – and gives us what is his – whole, forgiven, and righteous. I invite you to feel the power of the opposites in the trade Calvin describes. He writes:

> ... whatever is his may be called ours ... This is the wonderful exchange which, out of his measureless benevolence, he has made with us; that becoming Son of man with us, he has made us sons of God with him; that by his descent to earth, he has prepared an ascent to heaven for us; that, by taking on our mortality, he has conferred his immortality upon us; that accepting our weakness, he has strengthened us by his power; that receiving our poverty unto himself, he has transferred his wealth to us; that taking the weight of our iniquity upon himself (which oppressed us), he has clothed us with his righteousness.[1]

This miraculous trade occurs in the person of Christ. The one who is both fully God and fully man can effect the exchange that turns scarcity in the wilderness into a party of bounty. The Lord's Supper is a means whereby he brings this reality home to us week after week.

You give them something to eat

The Eucharist has been called an evangelical sacrament. We can see why from this story. For such an exchange as occurred in the feast in the desert is tremendously good news that can be joyously proclaimed to the world. The Church of Christ offers the miracle of this divine commerce wherever the bread is broken and the cup is raised. Our constant word to any and all who come is "You do not need to go away. Bring what you are to this table and trade it for what Christ has to give. Bring yourself, just as you are, and partake of him who gives himself to be known in this way. Do not go away discouraged that you are not worthy. Come and receive his worthiness."

We offer this feast of Christ's love as well when we leave our walls and go out into the world. We may follow the pattern of Jesus. After long periods of prayer, and so in constant communion with his Father, Jesus went abroad in the world. He went out to see whom he would see and then he met them with the love born of the Father, Son and Spirit. He had no formal program, no known timetables or strategy. Rather, he allowed himself to be interrupted. Postponing his need, he welcomed those whom he met. While we can never be Jesus, we may know that any love we will show must be born of our communion with the Lord of love. We must be connected to the source of feasts in the deserts if we are not to be overwhelmed by the need of the world. Then, we go to be available. We go forth to behold whoever comes into our path. And we regard them long enough for compassion to arise, for *heart-reaching* to occur. From that interaction of a living relationship to the Father and tender, regarding love for those before us, true Christian action arises. And miracles may occur.

Of course I am not saying that churches should not engage in planned, sustained work for spreading the gospel and bringing compassion to those in need. I do believe, however, that this story provides a grounding for our ministry that will keep it fresh and vital. Mission is born of our experience first as part of the needy crowd whom Jesus feeds. Then it flows from the realization that we are sent by Jesus to give others "something to eat." The telling of the Good News of the gospel in word and deed has its source in a deep communion with Christ. It has its effectiveness in the attentive beholding of others that links us to them from the heart.

With Jesus' *heart-reaching* for the multitude within us, we tell the story of his love and enact it with our compassion. We become hosts in his name. Attentively, we regard the needs and desires of our guests. Gratefully, we spread before them the banquet we are privileged to offer. For Christ has given himself to us, telling us that under no circumstances need we go away. And now he has sent us to host, to fete with joy, the hungry world. *They do not need to go away. You give them something to eat.* These words are the motto of Christ's house, the Church. Hosts in his name, we enact them literally and spiritually as we offer the multitudes the fullness of his gospel.

O*Father, we always seem to be unprepared for the demands of life. We find ourselves in the desert with no provision, and the blame is only ours. Yet you do not send us away. What a relief! You feed us from your own hand. Taking our poverty, you return to us your riches of grace. Taking our lack, you splash your abundance on us. Thank you. Send us now, we pray, to feed with food and love those who, like us, require your care. Amen.*

Endnote

1. John Calvin, *Institutes of the Christian Religion* (Philadelphia: Westminster Press, 1960), IV.xvii.2.

CHAPTER EIGHT

On the Contrary
Night Seas
Matthew 14:22-36

Take courage! It is I. Don't be afraid.
Matthew 14:27

In the dream, my vision was like a camera, zooming in from way above the scene. I burst from the realm of sleep into a night of wind and cold rain. Below me, a small boat seemed stationary in the heaving waves. The men with oars were drenched in rain and sea water. Now I could feel the cold. They were rowing against the wind and getting nowhere.

The wood on the boat looked very old. It was gray, and lined with vertical cracks. It seemed like wood on a seaside cottage from summers of years past. How old was this boat? In the logic of dream, the question brought the flash of understanding. This was the apostle's boat. This was the night Jesus walked on water to meet them. And I was there. No one noticed me. I was not out of place. "How can this be?" I wondered. "I am not worthy to be here. Soon Jesus will come, and I will see him. How can I possibly be here?"

I woke, but tried to follow the dream further. I was not worthy to be part of the story and yet there I was. These disciples, these experienced fishers, were tired and scared of the weather. They were preoccupied. When the figure appeared walking on the waves, their shouts were primal: long unchecked wails. Their relief at his voice brought them, and me, to tears. I wondered again, "How could I possibly be here?"

This sleepy meditation occurred after I had preached twice on this passage and shortly before I preached on it a third time. I have preached it at least three more times since then. Such repetition is rare for me. I usually like to move on to unmined texts. But something in this story of Jesus' walking on the waves has a powerful hold upon me. This mysterious story seems to offer such a deep metaphor for our spiritual experience with Jesus that I remain continually drawn to it.

It began with the account we considered in the last chapter. Jesus had fed, from five loaves and two fish, the thousands who had followed him into the desert. There had been a feast in the wilderness. Then the time came for Jesus to dismiss the disciples and the crowd. He had originally come to this desolate place to be alone. But for the sake of the crowd, he had postponed the meeting of that need. Now he would take time for prayer and recollection.

So Jesus made the disciples get into the boat and go before him to the other side of the lake. He stayed and dismissed the crowds. And after that he went up on the mountain by himself to pray. Jesus was there alone, while the disciples were out at sea. The gospel account tells us that when they had gone several miles from land, they were buffeted by the waves, for the wind was against them.

This story reveals a rhythm in being with Jesus, from separation to closeness to a time of separation again. The crowds who had found Jesus in the desert stayed for the feast, and then were dismissed. So we who experience a season of the deep, abiding presence of Jesus also experience seasons of being sent ahead, into dark seas and contrary winds.

Our story is silent about some questions it raises. Jesus sent them to the other side of the lake, but did he specify where they were to land? Why did he send them when night was at hand, instead of waiting until morning? My reading of a Bible Atlas indicates that their probable journey was around six miles. This shouldn't have taken more than a couple of hours. Yet, in our lesson, the wind and the waves are so bad that nearly eight hours after starting, the disciples are still in the middle of the lake. I wonder if even experienced fishers get frightened in seas like that. And I wonder what Jesus did all that time.

All of these questions are very much like any questions we would ask if we were being sent ahead. Where do you want me to go? Why am I leaving in the dark? What about the storm and when will you come on? And in our experience of being sent on ahead, over the waves, at the midnight hour and against the wind, such questions always remain unanswered. Only the reality of going on ahead, alone, is left.

Against the wind

For example, suppose you are working in a job you detest. You feel shriveled and shrinking there. You are stifled by your supervisor and lonely in the company of your co-workers. The moral climate is chilly, to say the best. So you feel called to move on, to leave the one thing the job has, security. You follow the prompting of the Spirit within you, and quit the job. You await the revelation of your life's true calling. Time passes; doors close. Children need to be educated. Mortgages need to be paid. Parents need to be taken care of. A cold wind blows against your face.

"You go on ahead to the other side," Jesus has said in effect, "And I will come to you." But what went unsaid was that the one hour journey could take all night; and the waves are high, the seas strong.

Or imagine that you have sold the house where you lived for much your life, raising children and sinking roots. You have given away many of the possessions that anchored you to the history of your life. And you have moved into a place that is smaller, comfortable, and well maintained by someone else. And then you realize it may be the last place you ever live. You become aware that you can no longer make your voice heard to those who supposedly work for you. They treat you like a child and think you don't notice when they ignore you. In a panic moment, the thought strikes that you have no way to get out; your freedom belongs to someone else.

"You go on ahead to the other side," Jesus says. "I will come to you." But first the wind will blow against you the whole of a dark night, and the waves will splash over you until you hardly remember what you're doing. Sometimes, for unapparent reasons, we are sent on ahead without the feeling of God's presence, and with the fear of the wind and waves.

Perhaps you have always dreamed of marriage, are wonderfully suited for companionship, but now, at 27, at 36, or 48, or 67 or 81, you are single. "You go on ahead to the other side." Perhaps once you found your partner for life, felt deeply contented, and now you are alone. "Go on ahead in the darkness."

The ghost of unmaking

And in the fourth watch, sometime between 3 and 6 a.m., Jesus finally came to them. He came walking on the sea, the master to his weary disciples. How they had waited for him! But when they saw him walking on the waves, they were terrified and cried out in fear, "It is a ghost!" (Matt. 14:26).

Yes, he comes, perhaps in the last watch of the night, in a way wholly unexpected. But he comes. Jesus walks across the troubled waters and arrives at the scene of our midnight fears. And yet, some nights we do not recognize him. Yearning for God, or at least for some sort of salvation from life's storm, we pray and pray. But when he finally arrives, we do not know who it is. And we are terrified by the very presence we prayed for.

The disciples thought Jesus was a ghost, some creature separated from his body, yet not with God in another realm. Some creature who might, if he touched them, separate them from their right minds. This was the fear of being undone. And so they had fear upon fear.

A man in middle age, with a good life and a respectable job, begins to make strange stops after work. He is restless, hoping for something. Several times a week, he hides his coat and tie in the trunk and goes in for a couple of beers at an overlooked pub across the river. He develops a new, alternate set of friends. They have no idea who he is in the daylight world.

Spinning the mug on the bar top, he drifts into thoughts of the trip to Nepal. He wants to go to a mystical place where his old life can be shed and his soul can soar. He wants to do the climbing, alone, that he has always dreamed of, before his body prevents him. But the work keeps hounding him. The work that seems more and more unreal.

One afternoon on his usual stool, he realizes how old his sons are now. And to think he was just about to teach them how to bat the ball … it was only yesterday, it was only eleven years ago and he can't remember the last time he looked into his wife's eyes, oh, what was she wearing this morning? And Jesus is coming to him across the waters of his life and he is terrified because he feels like he's coming undone. He is unraveling because everything he built his life upon has to be rethought. Everything he was proud of turned out to be an empire of sand. And where would he be if he left it all and turned back to those he loves? Would they have him now?

Do not be afraid

But immediately Jesus spoke to the disciples, "Take courage! It is I. Don't be afraid" (Matt. 14:27). The familiar voice cut through the noise of the wind and sliced through their fear. "It is I. Don't be afraid."

Perhaps you have known disquiet in your heart. There is a half-heard fear that what you once believed is no longer holding true. What once ordered your life with goals and boundaries is vanishing. The Spirit, from deep in your heart is rising with a new life in you. But right now it feels like death. The Spirit hints that the wave tossed night might end in morning's dawn, but first you must be undone. All those certainties, all that control, all that presumed power, needs to be ripped away by the sight of one who walks across the waves.

We are all sent out into the night, and sometimes all we have in the darkness is the vague hope that Jesus will come to us before the watch is through. And in every life there are times when Jesus does come, walking across the waves, ready to bring strength and calm. But the first sight of him is a threat, for his presence can unmake our lives. He changes us out there on the sea.

And we have in that night only the words, "Take heart. It is I. Do not be afraid."

Lo, it is *Jesu, the joy of our desiring.*

Lo, it is Jesus, *heart of my own heart.*

Lo, it is Jesus, *intercessor, friend of sinners, earth's redeemer* who pleads for me.

Even so, come Lord Jesus. Come to me in the darkness, unmake and remake my life. I cling but to the precious thought, "It is the Lord who comes in this night; I will not be afraid."

Meeting him on the water

This is one place to stop. Those in the dark night of storm might just want to meditate on this part. But the story goes on, and in our lives, there is another stage which occurs after we learn that everything is all right. There comes the call to do something preposterous and terrific.

With the wind still howling and the waves still high, Peter called out, "Lord, if it's you, tell me to come to you on the water" (Matt. 14:28). And Jesus said simply, "Come!" So, Peter got out of the boat.

He knew the risk. Peter fished for a living. He knew what chance one had stepping out of a boat into a dark and swelling sea. No one would hear his first cry. And what Peter wanted was so unnecessary. After all, he had already weathered the long midnight journey; he had survived the ghost of unmaking. Jesus was here now. Everything would be all right. All he had to do was stay in the boat. But he wanted more; and Jesus wanted to give it to him. Peter risked his life for something unnecessary but splendid.

And for a few, brief, glorious moments, he did it. Peter walked on the water toward Jesus. Of course, when he saw the wind and started to think about it, he got scared and began to sink. But he didn't hesitate to call out, "Lord save me!" (Matt. 14:30). Immediately Jesus reached out his hand and caught him. "You of little faith, why did you doubt?" (Matt. 14:31). Then both of them got into the boat, the wind ceased, and the night ended.

And the disciples fell down and worshiped Jesus.

What Peter did was not required. He could have thought, "Well, if it ain't broke, don't fix it." But I think Peter knew that Jesus calls us to something more. I suspect he might say, "Strive not just for what is necessary. Strive for the abundance to which I have called you. Fare forward for the risky frivolity of glory by which the universe was made."

Beyond necessity

The meaning of this story tells us that we are not here because we are necessary. Rather, we are here to adorn the glory of God as the overflowing abundance of his love that issued in creation. In the same way, the collection of God's people, the Church, does not exist because it is necessary. Yes, it is a haven in the dark night, a calm in the storm, but just as surely it exists to risk attempting to walk on the water. Not because it is necessary but because Jesus calls us to come to him over the waves. And that attempt, even if it fails, is what assures those in the dark night, and those coming undone with the presence of God that there is something worth hanging on for. There is a worship and a glory, and an abundance of life that arises out of the grim night. There is reason to hope.

But it may occur to us that such abundance is irregular. We may feel guilty for a robust spiritual life amidst the poverty of soul in our culture. In my dream about this passage, I felt unworthy to be part of the story. How could God call the likes of me to participate in such a great event? But then I realized that I was supposed to be there. It would have been a kind of reverse-pride to refuse. Some of us may be undertaking all kinds of ventures for the gospel, taking risks with money and time. But this expansion may make us feel frightened that we are not near the land; we are in the middle of the sea. There's no turning back. Are we doing too much? Will we have enough strength to carry on? Should we just take a nap in the back of the boat until dawn? Just when the Church and its people get going, we may grow afraid that walking on water is just not something people should do.

Guilt. Fear. Excessive pride. Fatigue. Complacency. These

emotions are natural, if we think too much about where we are in comparison to others, if we look at the waves instead of at Jesus. But we must not forget that it is Jesus who called us to get out of the boat. Jesus alone gives us the mission and the power to cross atop the sea. We do nothing on our own.

Yes, he calls us to a risky frivolity. And we are right in the middle of it. At any given time, different followers of Jesus are at all four places of the story. Some are rowing against the wind in the dark wondering if it will ever end. Some are coming undone with the changes God is making in them. Some are discovering the healing peace in the words, "It is I. Don't be afraid." And some are being called to get out of the boat and attempt new, risky things for God.

The people in the dark times need the strong to be risking new ways of love and service so that their abundant light will shine in the dark. Those of us who are in a season of strength need to hear those who are crying "It is a ghost!" so we can remember how important it is to share our comfort and our love. As the people of Christ, we hear Jesus together. When we are complacent, he says, "Go on to the other side." When we are ready to risk, he says, "Come to me." When we take our eyes off him to see guilt or pride or timidity, he says, "O people of little faith, why did you doubt?" When we are terrified, he says, "Take heart. It is I. Don't be afraid." In every season, though, whether we see him or not, he is there. In every hour he comes, and he still speaks.

Dear Jesus, you know how often we feel we have been sent ahead on contrary night seas without clear instruction. The winds of life blow hard against us. Come to us, dear Lord, with your life-transforming power. Even if it feels as if we will be undone by the change you bring, we want your presence. Make us more than we have been. Call us to come to you on the waves, in the confidence that you can save us. Speak to our hearts in every hour the blessed words, "It is I, don't be afraid." Amen.

CHAPTER NINE

Along the Way
Mark 8:27-38

But what about you? Who do you say that I am?

Mark 8:29

Near the midpoint of the gospels of Matthew, Mark and Luke, we come upon a pair of stories that are the hinge for the whole narrative of Jesus' days among us. Everything turns on them. Before these accounts, we hear of nearly three years of Jesus' ministry. The story moves at a breathless pace. After them, the gospels slow down and focus intently on the last months, and particularly the final days, of Jesus' life. The hinge is a remarkable week that begins with the moment Jesus first says that he knows he will have to suffer and die and concludes with the mysterious transfiguration on the mountain.

In Mark's gospel, the scene unfolds in an almost offhanded way. He writes, "Jesus and his disciples went on to the villages around Caesarea Philippi. On the way he asked them, 'Who do people say I am?'" (Mark 8:27). This was travel conversation. While they were en route to another place, when they were neither here nor there, Jesus just casually asked what the word was about him. The account has the feeling of the way something might just pop into your head while you're driving from one place to another. Having nothing urgent to talk about, you mention what's on your mind. There is time for reflection. How do you think we're doing? Who do people say that I am?

The reply was fascinating, "Some say John the Baptist; others say Elijah; and still others one of the prophets" (Mark 8:28). People were thinking of Jesus in terms of a great prophet returned to life. After all, Elijah had raised a boy from the dead and routed the prophets of Baal during the contest for Israel's soul on Mt. Carmel (see I Kings 18). This mighty man of God was last seen being taken "up to heaven in a whirlwind" (II Kings 2:11), and Scripture foretold that Elijah would come again to his people "before the great and dreadful day of the Lord" (Mal. 4:5). John the Baptist had drawn great crowds into the wilderness and rallied the people to prepare for God's savior of his people to arrive. John, as we saw last chapter, was a contemporary of Jesus who had only recently been martyred by King Herod, so that seems an odd designation for Jesus. In either case, however, Jesus was seen in terms of men who were known to the people, prophets who served God in powerful, yet mortal ways. These men were forerunners of the Lord, not the Lord himself. The popular word, then, was that Jesus was great, but he was still seen only in terms of those who had come before.

Then Jesus turned the discussions from general opinions to a pointed question, "But what about you? Who do you say that I am?" (Mark 8:29). That raises the stakes! It's one thing to talk about Jesus in a general way, but quite another to have to answer him personally. He called his disciples to a moment of confession. Peter seized the moment. He answered, "You are the Christ" (Mark 8:29). We have for so long associated the name of Jesus with the title of Christ that it may seem that Christ is simply his last name. It is hard to appreciate the daring in Peter's reply. He saw Jesus not as someone from the past returned, but as someone completely new. For centuries the Christ, the anointed one, the Messiah, had been longed for and expected. Great prophecies, such as those of Isaiah, had foretold of the coming of one who would redeem his people from bondage, both spiritually and materially. This Redeemer would restore them as God's beloved people and usher in days that could only be described as a new heaven and a new earth (Isa. 65:17). In fact, the coming of this savior was associated with the coming of God himself to shepherd his people (Isa. 62:11-12). So we can see why Matthew records a fuller response from Peter: "You are the Christ, the Son of the Living God" (Matt. 16:16). Peter reached beyond conventional understanding and human categories to recognize the significance of the one he followed.

Matthew alone records more of the conversation as we hear Jesus reply, "Blessed are you, Simon [Peter] son of Jonah, for this was not revealed to you by man, but by my Father in heaven" (Matt. 16:17). We are reminded of Jesus' words we considered in Chapter Two, "No one knows the Son except the Father, and no one knows the Father except the Son and those to whom the Son chooses to reveal him" (Matt. 11:27). We are not capable of grasping who Jesus is on our own. God cannot be known unless he reveals himself to us; neither can the Son of God be seen for all his significance without the supernatural aid of the Father.

Answering him from the heart

There is a difference between knowledge about Jesus that is external to our hearts and a knowing of him as the Son of God that fills our hearts even as it transforms them. As long as Jesus remains outside of us, our study is of no avail to our spiritual longing for rest and peace. Somehow, this information has to come within us. And Jesus told Peter that such knowing is a gift of God. It is a gift which requires our acceptance of it. When God shines the light in our hearts to see his glory in the face of Jesus Christ, he summons us not to remain indifferent, but to confess with Peter, "You are the Christ, the Son of the Living God!"

A book on the life of Jesus must, if it is to be faithful to the gospel presentation of Christ, contain a hinge much like the ones found in the New Testament. Jesus comes to us in every hour and circumstance of life. He comes all the way to where we are. But he will not come within without an invitation. There comes a moment when we must allow the knowledge to be made personal. Everything turns on our answer. Whether we will follow him through the second half of the gospels and the remainder of this book, depends on our reply. For eight chapters you, as readers, have been hearing what others say about who Jesus is. Now the time comes when Jesus directs the question to each of us, intimately and pointedly, "Who do you say I am?" How will you answer?

Perhaps some of what we have seen and heard will provide the frame for your reply:

- You are the one who calls me to rest when I am weary and heavy laden.

- You offer a fresh start when I have been years down the wrong road. I have been stuck at the tax booth, but you free me even as you call, "Follow me."

- You are the one who need only say the word and it will be done.

- You behold the grief of our lot and allow your heart to be moved. From your depths you say, "Don't cry," and offer a real hope of life eternal.

- When we are torn apart by the forces that grip us so closely, you set us free, clothing us and restoring us to our right minds.

- You tell us that no matter how inadequate we seem, we do not need to leave your company.

- You come across the waves in the dark night and assure us with your presence that we do not need to be afraid.

- You are the Christ, the Son of the living God, our brother, savior, friend and Lord.

Is the Holy Spirit resonating within your spirit that these words are true, that they indeed issue from your depths? Is God enabling you to make such a confession from your heart and with your lips? I pray even as I write that it will be so for you, my unknown reader in a faraway place. Across time and distance we may share a communion in the bond of knowing Jesus, truly and personally. Such a gift of grace he offers!

The dark turn

I wish the story ended there. But it is a hinge on which the gospels turn, and that turn is decidedly darker. As it was for Jesus and the disciples, so it remains two millennia later. Mark tells us that right after Peter's confession, Jesus "then began to teach them that the Son of Man must suffer many things and be rejected by the elders, chief priests and teachers of the law, and that he must be killed and after three days rise again. He spoke plainly about this ..." (Mark 8:31-32). Jesus came to bring healing, rest and new life. But the result of shining such light into the night of the world was a violent reaction of those whose darkened eyes burned at such startling illumination. Those whose slumber of rolling along with business as usual was disturbed lashed out at the light and tried to snuff it. We could not tolerate his presence among us, and Jesus knew his days were numbered.

In other words, the days of such gracious words and miracles were a foretaste of what was to come. They were not themselves the arrival of the banquet of God for all time. As we noted in Chapter Five, those who had been healed by Jesus would one day grow ill again. The little girl restored to life yet had to die again in this world. The Romans remained in power and, in fact, Israel's national life would get far worse (with the destruction of the temple in A.D. 70) than it had been. The Messiah was not making all things new completely and forever right then. His work was a sign that something had begun which was yet to be fulfilled. And the path to that fulfillment led through death before there could be resurrection.

Peter didn't care for this a bit. He had just made his stunning confession, and he meant it. He was ready for Jesus to be the glorious Christ prophesied in the Scriptures. It was time for God's people to rise to their promised place again. So he rebuked Jesus for such negative thoughts. Of course Peter had conveniently forgotten all the passages that indicated the terrible suffering the Messiah would endure to redeem his people (for example, Isaiah 53 and Psalm 22). Peter's words, then, echoed the temptation of the devil who had previously offered Jesus "all the kingdoms of the world and their splendor" (Matt. 4:8). Let's just skip the hard part and bring the kingdom of glory now.

Jesus reacted to him as if he were back on the mountain of temptation, "Out of my sight, Satan! You do not have in mind the things of God, but the things of men" (Mark 8:33). Jesus simply would not be distracted from his purpose. He knew that if he lived faithfully, he would be rejected. Jesus understood as well, however, that such defeat would ultimately lead to the victory of God over the forces of sin and death. But he had to make his way through the valley of the shadow first.

Now we can understand this, and even cheer Jesus on. Yes, please, go through the cross for our salvation! But the story darkens further with the summons to all who would confess him as Christ:

> If anyone would come after me, he must deny himself and take up his cross and follow me. For whoever wants to save his life will lose it, but whoever loses his life for me and the for the gospel will save it. What good is it for a man to gain the whole world, yet forfeit his soul? (Mark 8:34-36)

Yes, he comes with power and peace, rest and healing. He accepts us and restores us. He comes full of grace and love. But he also summons us to come after him in the way of death. There is just no way around this. Jesus does not simply restore us to the life we have chosen for ourselves, or make us able to follow our dreams. He did not enter the world to comfort us we hit snags pursuing our own ends. Jesus calls us to the way of the gospel, and though it leads to the deepest fulfillment of our humanity, it also involves a death to self.

The new and living way

Someone has said, "When Christ calls a man to follow him, he bids him come and die." The gift of faith, the sacraments of baptism and Holy Communion, times of prayer and the hearing of the Word are all ways Christ unites us to himself. When we are joined to Christ, we are joined to his death. As he died to sin, we have died to sin in him, and must continue to do so. But also, thankfully, as he rose and lives at the right hand of God, so we too have his life-giving Spirit in us and have risen with him. We are called to continue in new life, by our choice and his power.

Andrew Murray, commenting on the phrase that Jesus has made for us "a new and living way" (Heb. 10:20), writes:

> The new and living way ... We know now what it is: it is the way of death.
>
> Yes, the way of death is the way of life. The only way to be free from our fallen nature, with the curse and power of sin resting on it, is to die to it. Jesus denied Himself, would do nothing to please that nature He had taken, sinless though it was in Him. He denied it; He died to it. This was to Him the path of life. And this is to us the living way. As we know Him in the power of His resurrection, He leads us into the conformity to His death. He does it in the power of the Holy Spirit. So His death and His life, the new death and the new life of deliverance from sin, and fellowship with God, which He inaugurated, work in us, and we are borne along as He was to where He is.[1]

Though Christ lives in us, we yet have a sinful nature with which we must struggle all our days on this earth. The only way to succeed is to find and actively take our place in Christ, dead to sin and alive to God. Through the years, he leads us to die more and more to self that we might grow more and more like him.

The apostle Paul intimately understood this spiritual reality. He was literally stopped in his tracks by a vision of the risen Christ. His old life ended. Once he had been a persecutor of Christians; then he became the champion of the gospel. He had known earthly success in education, heritage and spirituality. But all of those things lost their appeal to him. Hear how he considers the trade, "But whatever was to my profit, I now consider loss. What is more, I consider everything a loss compared to the sur-passing greatness of knowing Christ Jesus my Lord for whose I have lost all things. I consider them rubbish, that I may gain Christ and be found in him ..." (Phil. 3:7-9). Elsewhere he says, "I die every day" (I Cor. 15:31). He let everything else go and found the pearl of great price. Losing his life, he found it in Christ.

So we will have crosses to bear. There will be the suffering of daily living in a world such as this. There will be the painful consequences of our sinfulness, and the awareness of this will be more acute the more we know Jesus. And there will be the fallout of our association with Jesus. Sooner or later, if we are walking in the light, those in the dark will lash out.

Though we leave the "tax booths" for a new life, there will be the old friends to deal with, both temptation and opportunity. Though we find healing in body, relationships, mind and soul, there will be conflicts and illnesses to face. Though Jesus sets us free from powers of destruction, they will try to bind us again. We are on the earth-side of the kingdom of heaven still. Jesus has given us a foretaste of what is to come. The Spirit within us guarantees with the peace that passes understanding that there is joy now and much, much more to come. But we must yet struggle. The way is hard and full of tribulation. This is just the way it is.

The gospel of John does not contain the scene we have been considering. Yet, it has a parallel moment of questioning and reply. John records that after hearing some of Jesus' hard sayings, "many of his disciples turned back and no longer followed him" (John 6:66). Jesus then turned to the Twelve, his closest friends, and asked, "You do not want to leave too, do you?" (John 6:67). Again it was Simon Peter who had the boldest reply of faith. "Lord, to whom shall we go? You have the words of eternal life. We believe and have come to know that you are the Holy One of God" (John 6:68-9).

To whom shall we go? If there were someone else, someone easier to follow who could still deliver the same love, we might well leave Jesus. If there were a better rest for our weariness of soul, a surer hope of life amidst all this death, we surely might leave this demanding Jesus. But Peter pegged it: You have the words of eternal life. There is no way around death. We are dead spiritually without Jesus. This world is full of dying we cannot avoid. To choose Jesus is to die to sin and self. It involves voluntarily entering more pain and death than the world in the present moment demands. But the other side of such an offering is life, glorious eternal life that flows from the center of being. And we may taste of it and live in the joy of it right now.

This Jesus who comes to us ever sharpens the questions to a fine point: "Who do you say that I am? You do not want to leave, too, do you?" The soul cries out with a reply. If by grace we are led to confess him, then we know we will enter the way of death with him, death to self and sin. To make the step, we must have the hope of resurrection and life set before us. Thankfully, the second story in this hinge that is the turning point of the gospels will offer us a glimpse of just such an eternal, powerful life.

Your question stabs right to the heart, Jesus. Who do we say you are? We long to make a confession as bold as Peter's. But we also know the cost. You come to us and offer everything. Though we have nothing to offer you, yet you ask for our wills and our allegiance. You ask us to die with you to self that we might live to God. We can only make such a step with your power enabling us. Though it frightens us, we nevertheless ask, come within and quicken our hearts. Help us believe and confess, You are the Christ, the Son of the Living God! Amen.

Endnote

1. Andrew Murray, *The Holiest of All* (Springdale, Pa.: Whitaker House, 1996), p. 364.

CHAPTER TEN

In a Shining Moment

Mark 9:2-13

This is my Son, whom I love. Listen to him!

Mark 9:7

If you were staging the gospels in two acts, where would you put the intermission? I might be inclined to break right after Simon Peter's triumphant declaration, "You are the Christ, the Son of the Living God." The music could swell as the curtain closed, and the audience could get up with a sense of joy. But as we saw in the last chapter, Jesus would not let the scene end there. He darkened the mood with his predictions of suffering ahead, which his disciples must be willing to share. That would end the act with a foreshadowing of doom.

And for most of the people around Jesus, that is how the first half of the gospel closed. But while the crowds were out in the lobby for the leftover bread and fish, trying to understand this dark plot twist, something crucially important was happening off-stage. Three of the disciples were taken with Jesus to a high mountain for a day set apart from everyone else. An event that has come to be known as the *transfiguration* occurred during what seemed to be an intermission in the gospel drama.

Jesus took Peter, James and John up a mountain whose name is not specifically mentioned. Near the peak, Jesus suddenly began to shine. Each gospel writer contributes to the description of this otherworldly event. Matthew says that Jesus' face "shone like the sun, and his clothes became white as the light" (Matt. 17:2). In Mark, Jesus' robes became "dazzling white, whiter than anyone in the world could bleach them" (Mark 9:3). And Luke describes them as "bright as a flash of lightning" (Luke 9:29). Through the centuries, the Church has understood that all these phrases are metaphorical descriptions of a real event that is beyond articulation. The gospel writers point us toward a glory that pale human words can never adequately render.

On the mountain, the divine nature of Jesus shone through his human body. The curtain between heaven and earth was pulled back so that something of the splendor of the eternal Son of God was revealed. During most of his days with us, Jesus showed the emptying of God, his humbling, by limiting himself to the confines of our humanity. But the transfiguration briefly revealed his true glory. It portended the raising up of our humanity in Christ. And it would later be seen as a foretaste of how Christ will return to the earth in lordly power. This was a moment when it became clear to the witnesses that Jesus was far more than a mere man. There was a shining splendor in him, veiled most of the time by flesh, but now revealed for a moment as a confirmation of who he is and a sign of what is to come.

Commentators through the years have noted that the transfiguration reveals the voluntary nature of Christ's suffering. He was not taken to the cross against his will. No human, or for that matter, no spiritual power could have bound and killed Jesus without his consent. He is the Son of his Father, and that relationship is eternal. It sustains the universe. There is no greater power or higher authority. At any moment, the human Jesus had at his disposal the resources of his divinity. So he entered his passion and laid down his life for us absolutely willingly. He endured every moment of temptation and agony with the further tempting knowledge that he could have ended the suffering instantly. The glory of the transfiguration is a window, then, on the depths of God's loving condescension to us.

At the same time, however, the transfiguration was an event of strengthening for Jesus in his humanity. The fact that it occurred away from the crowds, with only three witnesses, indicates that its primary significance was for Jesus. Right after he articulated, perhaps for the first time, that he must suffer and die, this moment of confirmation was given to him. While Jesus had constant communion with his Father, we do not know the exact extent of his consciousness of his divinity throughout his years with us. Scripture does not describe the interplay between the human nature and the God-nature in Christ. It could be that he knew all along the precise form that the end of his life would take. Or it could be that this knowledge unfolded for him during these last weeks. In any case, the moment of naming aloud his forthcoming suffering was accompanied with a steely resolve to see his work through to the end. (Luke tells us in Luke 9:51 how soon after this Jesus "set his face" to go to Jerusalem.) And his faithfulness was followed by a heavenly response on the mountain of transfiguration.

Visitors from the past

The gospels tell us that Moses and Elijah appeared to him. They spoke with Jesus "about his departure, which he was about to bring to fulfillment at Jerusalem" (Luke 9:31). Why these two? There seem to be several reasons. Moses represented God's redemption and the giving of the law. It was Moses who led the people out of slavery in Egypt through the parted waters of the Red Sea. And he was the one who received from God the Ten Commandments on the stone tablets upon Mt. Sinai. As we noted in the last chapter, Elijah represented all the prophets who had ever called Israel back to faithfulness. He had defeated the prophets of Baal upon Mount Carmel and led the people to reaffirm their allegiance to the Lord. Moreover, both men had had striking experiences of the presence of the Lord. Not only had Moses heard God speaking in the burning bush, but God had revealed the sacred name, I AM, to Moses (Ex. 3:14). And, Elijah, hiding in a cave on a mountainside, had heard the Lord speak, not in whirlwind or fire, but in the "gentle whisper" (I Kings 19:12).

Can you imagine the conversation they had with Jesus? Of course all speculation fails us. But consider what Jesus the man might have wanted to ask. "Moses, how did you stand it when you came down from the mountain and found the people worshipping the golden calf? It's so hard to see their unbelief after all I say and do. How did you go on? Elijah, were you ever frightened that day on Mt. Carmel? Did you wonder if God might not actually light the altar you had doused with water? The way ahead is very difficult for me. Every step is a strain now. Elijah, did the whisper give you enough assurance? Look, these disciples are no help. See how they've gone asleep. Can you help me?"

The transfiguration offers this alternating between a revelation of Christ's glory and a touching glimpse of his true humanity. He had the stature to converse without fear with the greatest of the prophets. Yet, their presence and their counsel was a needed comfort. He knew the splendor of his life with the Father as God; yet as a man who walked amidst the constraints of body and time, he cherished the repeated affirmation from above.

Imaginative interactions

Though this mystical experience of Jesus seems far removed from daily life, there are more connections than we might at first realize. Jesus had direct access to Elijah and Moses that we do not. Yet, we may "consult" with biblical characters as well as saints from our lives if we employ our sacred imaginations. We ask such connecting phrases in ordinary conversation. Sometimes it's pejorative: "Why, what do you think your great Aunt Mary would say if she saw you doing that?" Other times, it's reassuring, "If only your father could see you now. He would be so proud." In making decisions, bereaved spouses in particular might ask, "What would my husband have done in this situation? How would my wife have decided this matter?" Without at all implying any sort of occult practice, we all may use our imaginations to gain the perspectives of others.

My grandfather was also a Presbyterian minister. I often wonder how he conducted his life and ministry in a way that made him so highly regarded. He died when I was five, so my memories of him are certainly not professional ones. I'd like to know how he balanced ministry with family responsibilities and church life with his head for business. I often think of him when I am in long ecclesiastical meetings and wonder how he got through them. And how did he preach so simply and to the heart without compromising his scholarship?

I received a precious insight into his life several years ago when I had a visit with a woman who used to be my nanny years ago. I asked her what he was like. "Oh, he used to walk you up and down the house," she said. "He'd sing, or sometimes he'd just be quiet. I guess he was praying for you." I was glad she was busy with the dishes as we talked, because I couldn't hide my tears. Every once and a while I need to consult that vision, for reassurance and for direction in what's important during these busy days. Perhaps you, too, have some people in your memory who offer guidance and a steady hand.

Moreover, we may interact with the biblical characters far more intimately than we may realize. When we have learned their stories and studied their personalities, strengths and weaknesses, we may use our imaginations to inquire further of them. The texts of Scripture provide boundaries to safeguard us from foolish or dangerous speculation, while within those outlines there is much room for exploration. We could, for instance, go back to some of the characters we've studied in this book. We might ask Levi, "Did it worry you just to leave your job unattended? I'd like to start a new life with Jesus as you did, but I worry about the cost."

How do you imagine Levi replying? Perhaps he would answer that walking away from a Roman responsibility did indeed make him look over his shoulder, though once down the road with Jesus, so many other concerns came up that his previous job paled in significance. And that might instruct you, if you are able, not to leave loose ends in your affairs as your life with Jesus deepens. Or Levi's story might free you from a feeling of slavery to work to re-prioritize what is most important.

We might ask the widow of Nain what is was like to meet Jesus in the midst of grief. Could she feel Jesus *heart-reaching* toward her before he raised her son? What was he like as he regarded her? And perhaps she would tell us that even before he called back her boy, she knew that all was well. In the sorrow on his face was an understanding that filled her loneliness even in that moment. By the command of his voice, she knew that there is so much more life than we see here. And so this widow might be a companion to us who wait in grief for brighter days to come. She might connect us more fully to Jesus.

For an event so different from daily experience, the transfiguration has much to tell us of the way Jesus comes to us now. He speaks, still, through the accounts of the people he touched long ago. What he did for them, how he felt with them, can be for us as well. Even as he was linked to Elijah and Moses, we may, at a lesser level, be linked to the people of the Bible. But more, because we are united to Christ by his love in the power of the Holy Spirit, the rest of the transfiguration experience has something to say to us as well.

A word from the Father

On the mountain, Jesus received much more than a consultation with the prophets of old. Soon after their appearance, a bright cloud moved over them. It covered the mountain top, and from it came a voice saying, "This is my Son, whom I love! Listen to him!" (Mark 9:7). The Father spoke an audible word of confirmation to his Son Jesus.

Such a voice had been heard once before. When the time came for Jesus to begin his public ministry, he went to John at the Jordan River. Upon entering the waters, he submitted to a sinner's baptism. It was a decisive moment when the sinless one identified himself with us. He acted on our behalf, taking a sinner's place in the river. And when he came out of the water, his action was ratified. The Holy Spirit descended on him in the form of a dove. And a voice came from heaven, "You are my Son, whom I love; with you I am well pleased" (Mark 1:11). The three persons of the Triune God were thus involved: incarnate Son, descending Spirit and speaking Father.

Now, a similarly crucial decision had been made. Jesus would not avoid the path of suffering but would go through it. Still sinless, he would do more than accept a symbolic death in baptism for sinners. He would undergo a literal death for us. And in response came the word from his Father, "This is my Son!" His Father ratified his decision and spoke to strengthen him for the days ahead. In the covering of the cloud, the Church for centuries has seen the presence of the Spirit, thus making this a second moment when the three persons of the one God were seen at work. The incarnate Son stood on the mountain; the Holy Spirit descended on him in the cloud; and the speaking Father confirmed his identity with audible words.

As far removed from us as the transfiguration seems, we may nevertheless see in it an important spiritual dynamic that still holds true. Consider the emotions associated with needing to make a major, difficult decision. You are seeking to know and to have the courage to follow the will of God in your life. But before the resolution comes, you feel drained of energy. It may seem that you are moving in slow motion, heavy with brooding. Even when you are not consciously weighing the decision, your mind and soul are working on the problem. Life is in crisis; you are at a crossroads and seemed blocked from knowing which path to take.

At last the answer comes. It may surface from within after prayer and reflection. It may come in the words of a confidant which suddenly strike you as a message from God. It may hit you in a seemingly random accident after which you say, "Of course. It all seems so obvious now." So you make a decision to enact a particular action trusting that this is God's desire. You strike out on the new path and now the way that seemed hopelessly blocked opens up easily. Light shines; energy returns. You enter a wonderful, almost paradoxical period of what may be described as *vibrant peace.*

Perhaps it's the day you finally decide, "I'm going to leave this job and try a new career path; I'm not going to slog through a comfortable routine any longer just to be safe. Now is the time." And so you let the music, the design, the computer program, the business idea, or whatever it is finally come forth. Or maybe you realize, "I've got to stay; I've got to quit looking around and take these relationships seriously again. I know where I belong. It's time to stop flirting with disaster and get down to the work of faithfulness." Or perhaps you decide to stop struggling and open the door to the Spirit of Christ who has been knocking steadily on your heart. His hand has been heavy upon you and finally you look up and say Yes. Whatever the situation, when we finally resolve to go down the path of God's leading, and take a step, then confirmation comes.

We can actually see people transfigured when they take such steps. Their faces change; the furrowed muscles relax. They walk more sprightly. Peace comes and their eyes are clear. Inertia and inactivity become a robust productivity. Confidence returns to the voice. Life has changed.

The German author Goethe described this spiritual dynamic:

> Until one is committed, there is hesitancy, the chance to draw back, always ineffectiveness. Concerning all acts of initiative (and creation), there is one elementary truth, the ignorance of which kills countless ideas and splendid plans: that the moment one definitely commits oneself, then Providence moves too.
>
> All sorts of things occur to help one that would never otherwise have occurred. A whole stream of events issues from the decision, raising in one's favor all manner of unforeseen incidents and meetings and material assistance, which no one could have dreamed would have come his way. Whatever you can do, or dream you can, begin it. Boldness has genius, power, and magic in it. Begin it now.

The transfiguration seems to have followed from Jesus' resolute commitment to follow the faithful path of suffering. From the voicing of that choice, came an event "which no one would have dreamed could come his way," a moment of significance not only for Jesus then, but for the entire body of his people as they have waited for his return throughout the centuries.

The sign of what will be

As the followers of Christ have suffered in this mortal, brutal world, they have always held hard to the promise that Jesus will come again in glory to judge the world and usher in the dawning of a new heaven and a new earth. Near the end of his life, Peter reflected on what it meant to have been with Jesus on the mountain that day. He writes:

> We did not follow cleverly invented stories when we told you about the power and coming of our Lord Jesus Christ, but we were eyewitnesses of his majesty. For he received honor and glory from God the Father when the voice came to him from the Majestic Glory, saying, "This is my Son, whom I love; with him I am well pleased." We ourselves heard this voice that came from heaven when we were with him on the sacred mountain. (II Peter 1:16-18)

In the moment, Peter had been overwhelmed by the transfiguration. Ancient paintings depict the disciples knocked on their heads by this appearance of glory. But years later, Peter understood more. The transfiguration was a guarantee of the "coming of our Lord Jesus Christ." The shining cloud and the voice of the Father not only assured Jesus. They reverberated in the hearts and preaching of the disciples as a unique historical event, so beyond anything they could have invented that it provided a bedrock of assurance in times of trial.

The dark turn of the gospels in Christ's prediction of his death, then, gave way to the shining glory on the mountain. Suffering was inevitable for Jesus, and his followers have to walk that road as well. But the transfiguration offered a glimpse of the other side of the passion. There would be resurrection, and more, there will yet be a return to the world in glory. As Hebrews enjoins us, "Let us fix our eyes on Jesus, the author and perfecter of our faith, who for the joy set before him endured the cross ..." (Heb. 12:2). We have a hope so great that we can scarcely describe it. The kingdom of God has been secured by Jesus, and its full glory will soon be revealed. We who are in Christ share his life now. This one who took our humanity upon himself is our brother, and through him we are children of his Father. So in Christ, the word on the mountain is for us. God says to us, "In Christ Jesus, you are my beloved child with whom I am pleased!"

The transfiguration, then, cannot be relegated to an offstage event during the intermission of the gospel drama. News of this significance belongs on center stage, the beginning and guarantee of the final glorious act.

———————————◆———————————

W e thank you for the gift of the transfiguration, for a moment when you allowed your glory to be glimpsed by human eyes. We're relieved to know you received some comfort before your suffering, Lord Jesus. And how grateful we are for the confirmations you give to us. Thank you, Father, for including us in Christ as your beloved sons and daughters. The way of the cross and the death of self is hard, but we are cheered to know that even as we take our halting steps along that path, your voice sounds and your Spirit is poured out. Amen.

CHAPTER ELEVEN

Asking What We Want

Luke 18:35-42

Jesus stopped and said, "Call him."

Mark 10:49

Right as he came down from the mountain of transfiguration, Jesus encountered a boy afflicted by violent seizures. Jesus healed the boy (when his other disciples had not been able to during his absence) by exorcising a demon. After this episode, the gospel writers turn their attention to Jesus' teachings and his conflicts with the religious leaders. Then, just prior Palm Sunday, they pick up the stories of the last people to begin following Jesus before his passion. These final disciples get in just under the wire, and so their stories are important to us who may yet be wrestling with the question, "Who do you say that I am?" It seems no accident that after the supposedly enlightened teachers of the law had failed to see who Jesus was, we read of a blind man crying out in faith.

He was a familiar sight, pleading every day for coins along the Jericho Road. So familiar, in fact, that he was easily overlooked, as quickly passed as the town drunk or the usual gang of bridge dwellers. That's why they brought him to the highway, where he could beg from travelers and newcomers. But that meant that he was also subject to robbers who would stoop so low as to steal from the blind, and to the jeers of people who enjoyed seeing someone beneath themselves. Such was the life of a blind man, nameless in Luke's telling of the story, but called Bartimaeus in Mark.

He spread out his cloak in the dust, perhaps put a few "sample" coins out so people would get the idea of the right amount. Listening for the sounds of animals and travelers on the road, Bartimaeus learned to judge the most effective distance to begin his pleas. And he begged, "Alms for a blind man! Coins for the poor!" Sometimes a coin clinked into his cloak. Other times a foot followed a curse, "Why don't you work like the rest of us?" Sometimes the coins bounced off him or landed beyond easy reach and he had to search for them, groping in the dirt and dust.

The man did a lot of listening. He knew from sounds what kind of people were passing by. And after Bartimaeus had pronounced his litany, he listened to the conversations of those that passed. Lately, there had been a lot of talk about Jesus, the rabbi from Nazareth. The blind man paid attention to news that might affect him, and rumors had reached him that Jesus could make leprous skin clean and smooth again. He could silence the madness of demons, loose the paralyzed limbs, even raise the dead. Bartimaeus felt that if he could just get Jesus' attention, then he could be healed.

He would not be silenced

Bartimaeus was used to begging. He was used to being ignored or insulted. He was also desperate. When he heard the sounds of an unusually huge crowd passing and found out that Jesus himself was passing by, he didn't hesitate: "Jesus, Son of David, have mercy on me!" (Mark 10:47).

Imagine you were escorting a prominent religious figure through your town. And suppose the town character ran up to him, "Coz, can I talk to you a minute? Com'on, just a word?" Would you politely introduce the two? Or would you, like me, be embarrassed that the advance team didn't do their job to clear the streets? Wouldn't you say something about your guest's stature and requirements, then try to move on? The disciples wanted no interference from the city beggar. They told him bluntly to shut up.

An inner debate raced through the blind man's head in an instant: "Embarrass yourself now, and what few coins you get will be cut off. You might even be harmed. Maybe it would be better just to take your place. Accept your lot. Make do with what you have. And yet, maybe this is the moment. One shot. Jesus is here now and may never be again. You could be well, if you could get to him, and then what does it matter what they think?" Hope won the argument and Bartimaeus shouted all the more, "Son of David, have mercy on me!" (Mark 10:48). It was shrill and obnoxious.

But Jesus heard him and stopped. And so the crowd halted and all the noise hushed. Time and the world froze. Jesus said simply "Call him" (Mark 10:49). So the disciples summoned Bartimaeus. The blind man immediately leapt up, leaving his coins and his cloak. There was no turning back. Jesus asked him, "What do you want me to do for you?" (Mark 10:51). For half a second, perhaps, the blind man thought, "What a strange question! What else could I want? Don't you see who I am?" But the moment was now and he didn't hesitate. "Rabbi, I want to see" (Mark 10:51).

We hardly need to tell the rest of the story. The climax has passed. The outcome is sure. "Receive your sight; your faith has healed you" (Luke 18:42). And immediately the blind man was the seeing man. And he never went back for his coins. He followed Jesus, praising God, and so did everyone else.

The faith that heals

"Your faith has healed you." What was Bartimaeus' faith? First, he cried out to Jesus for mercy. He understood the connection between his need and the man from Nazareth. This Jesus was the Son of David, the Messiah, Israel's hope. He was the one to go to with overwhelming need. And so the blind man had prayed. Not quietly and reverently, but from his guts, with a loud voice. Jesus, have mercy on me!

At this point in the gospels as well as this point in the book, the questions get more intense. We are approaching the end, and so we ask pointedly: Have you ever cried out to Jesus that way?

Right out of the very center of you, as if you had no choice, because your need was so great and you realized that only Jesus could help. You knew that you were not worthy, and could make no claim on him. Only if he regarded upon you with mercy would he ever help you. And your need pushed you to ask for grace you didn't deserve, based solely on the graciousness of Jesus to whom you cried out.

If you've been in the tank, you've prayed that way. There are many other metaphors. If you've crashed through the branches and brambles and hit the ground in a heap, you understand Bartimaeus. If you've spent three days and nights in the belly of the whale, you've prayed as he did. If God was gracious enough to let you hit bottom before you died, then at last all the junk, all the trappings, all the pretensions were cleared away and raw need pierced through a voice that had nothing left but faith, "Jesus, have mercy on me!"

But people don't care much for that kind of faith. The blind man isn't someone you would take to the club for lunch. He was far too raw, too demonstrative. He wasn't someone that would make us comfortable. Bartimaeus looked like a fanatic. He wasn't someone who would be comfortable in many of our churches. Why, he'd have his hands up in the air, and he'd make noise when he prayed, and, well, it just wouldn't work. The disciples now as well as then want to silence the shouts of desperate faith.

Have you ever felt that way? Perhaps you have questions. Hurting, burning questions. But perhaps you've found that you can't ask them in the company of Christ's people. Oh, everyone else has them too, but since there aren't easy answers, it's as if we've all entered an agreement not to ask them. And if you do raise painful issues, people get very uncomfortable.

As Jesus indicted the Pharisees of his time, and even his own disciples, so we realize that it is the very people of Christ, his Church, who stifle the blind Bartimaeus on the roadside of our sanctuaries. We have great gaping needs in our lives and we come to church desperate for God but find that God is muffled and muted by so much baggage. Our worship is so encumbered by unwritten codes, about what time it is, about putting on a game face for each other, about keeping it together, about staying within the lines. Sometimes I just want to come out of the pulpit into my congregation and shout, We're talking about God here! We're talking what really matters! Jesus Christ is the most important person in the universe, and we've got him managed and boxed and packaged to the point that we're spiritually impoverished. Like Bartimaeus, we may need to shake free of the old strictures to get to Jesus, the real, vibrant Jesus so often obscured by his own people.

The blind man had the courage to shout all the more after people told him to be quiet. Bartimaeus risked being called a fanatic at work to speak about Jesus. He dared having his neighbors think he'd gone crazy because he finally realized the only thing that matters in life. And he fairly invited his old friends to laugh at him for the change in his life. He risked it all, because he just wouldn't be shut up.

The blind man left his coins and his way of life behind. He gambled it all that Jesus would be who he seemed to be. There's always a risk in faith. It can paralyze us. For we might well be disappointed. We might be embarrassed or find ourselves left alone. Or, of course, we just might end up healed, set free and filled with joy.

If Jesus Christ is really the Lord, the Lord of the universe, the only one who really matters, then what are we doing sitting in the dust counting the few coins that have fallen into our filthy cloaks? At the end of the day, will we say to God, "Look at this stack of coins I collected with my life. Best beggar in town." And will God reply, "I had everlasting life for you. I had sight for the blind, water for the thirsty, hope for the hopeless. And all you have are beggar's coins?" The faith of Bartimaeus, the faith that heals, grabs hold of Jesus and does not let go.

What do you want?

The blind man risked it all to get to Jesus. And when he did, Jesus asked him, "What do you want me to do for you?" That's such a tender question from the savior. He refused to define the blind man's life by his blindness. He saw the whole man, the entire life, with all its possibilities. What do you want? Jesus knew what Bartimaeus wanted. God knows what we want. But somehow, our naming it is very important to God.

So what would you say? If you had one moment, one request before Jesus, what would it be?

Our first impulse might be to treat the question as an Aladdin's Lamp. We might ask for something on the order of Bartimaeus' request for sight. There are loved ones who are ill, dear ones off on dangerous paths, hearts that are broken, and people all over living in desperate straits. God certainly hears these requests, but I have never been able to discern a pattern in the rare times when dramatic answers occur. In fact, it seems that usually Christians must suffer the trials of living and dying just like the rest of the world. Most often, God works from the inside out. Jesus' miracles were a concentrated expression of his power. Such power can still be exercised, but usually God's ways are quieter and less apparent.

If the usual way of life is granted, then how would you answer the question? What do you want in the depths of your soul?

I believe that God gives us his Spirit without measure. He answers our desperate thirsty cries with living water. When the hungry, famished heart at last cries out that it cannot feed itself, God rushes in with the bread of life. When we beg for mercy, he pours in our hearts the amazing grace of forgiveness. When we answer the knock on the door to our lonely, guilty, battered souls, Jesus and his Father come in and take up residence and invite us into their wonderful life of love and communion.

Psalm 42 begins, "As the deer pants for the streams of water, so my soul pants for you, O God. My soul thirsts for God, for the living God." What we most want is God himself. Connected to him, the rest of life unfolds with a sense of peace, whether our requests are answered with abundant bounty or baffling scarcity. With God poured out in our hearts "by the Holy Spirit whom he has given us" (Rom. 5:5), joy flows from the inner depths into the outer, daily life. Our truest desire, when all the layers are pealed away and the essence of humanity is revealed, is for fellowship with God. Everything else issues from that center. Will you and I risk asking Christ for nothing less than himself?

Sent

Now before we leave this story, there is one more angle to take. Many of you who have read this far in this kind of book will be people who have already come to know Jesus Christ in a deeply meaningful way. For all our sinfulness and all our muffling and distractions, God has gotten the message about his Son through to us. We have experienced the communion of personal prayer. We know what it is to be in the company of fellow believers. We have feasted at the banquet table of grace. Jesus has called us to follow him, and we have been willing. So we know that Jesus asks more of us than reveling in his presence. He sends us out, out from our homes and churches, and into the world.

In the new day, when you have put the book down, you will encounter the people shouting at you, clamoring for attention, for money, for time, for love. None of us can help every single one. But I believe that God calls to each one of us through the needs of particular people who are our particular bundle of care. The blind man is out there, shouting for Jesus. If we are too busy with our own pursuits, we will want to silence him. Why, we can barely get any time with Jesus ourselves for all there is to do. But we must be careful that we haven't busied ourselves right out of the work God has for us to do.

The blind man is on the roadside crying for mercy. We are not to answer every cry. But also, we are not to ignore every cry. Some of those cries have our names attached to them. To some, you and I are called, in the name of Jesus, to say, "What do you want me to do for you?"

Not many of us will be able literally to open the eyes of the blind or end human abuse or banish need. But our very question of availability, "What do you want me to do for you?" will open the way for Jesus' love to reach people. Our very stopping to notice and to inquire and to care will let the rivers of living water out of the dam and into the hearts.

Perhaps it is time for us to be messier in our faith. With

Bartimaeus as our example, we may stop pretending we can make it on our own. Rather than continuing to try to do it all ourselves, we may raise our heartcries to God. We may attach our deepest needs to the savior who stops when he hears the anguished cries of the soul. It wouldn't be a bad thing if there was a little more crying and shouting in our prayers and in our churches.

So we will risk asking those in pain, "What do you want me to do for you?" We may not be able to handle the request. We may have to come face to face with the agony of life on this earth, with no solutions but the love that cares in the midst of suffering. That's all right. The cure and the salvation are Jesus' work. It's our availability to others that opens a path for him to do it.

When God came all the way down to be with us, he came as the kind of man who noticed those who were usually ignored. Jesus had ears attuned to their cries even when others were shouting them down. That means there's hope for the likes of us. He won't pass us by. He won't be too busy or uninterested. He sees us, even with weak voice, in the back of the crowd, blind, begging, with nothing to offer. And he stops. He stops for each one of us and asks, "What do you want me to do for you?" Jesus yearns to give us what we most need, our heart's truest desire. He longs to give us himself.

---

*S*on of David, have mercy on us! Do not pass us by! Do not let others silence us. O Jesus, notice our need. It is for you. Fill us with yourself. Come to us in our poverty and blindness and give us sight to see the riches we have in you. Then send us, we pray to those in need along the roadside. For we would not be the final resting place of your bountiful love, but its everflowing conduit. Amen.

CHAPTER TWELVE

Seeking What Was Lost
Luke 19:1-10

> *Jesus said to him, "Today salvation has come*
> *to this house, because this man, too, is a*
> *son of Abraham. For the Son of Man came*
> *to seek and to save what was lost."*
>
> Luke 19:9-10

A long time ago, a friend was in bad shape. He had been blindsided by his wife's departure for another. Already he had shuffled his career for her sake and now the future looked bleak on every front. He was a shell of his former self, a wounded man. In such a state, he went out of loyalty to the wedding of a colleague. As if watching others' joy in married love wouldn't be depressing enough, he arrived at the festivities physically ill. Sick, gaunt, stunned, miserable – he seemed a wreck.

But a woman at the wedding saw something else. She saw an intelligent, attractive man with great depth of soul and passion for life. He wasn't looking for a relationship, or even comfort. She wasn't acting out of pity. She saw him and fell in love. She saw something in him that she wanted, some essential quality that she desired so deeply that she could ignore all the flaws that kept others at a distance. And her love transformed his life. Very soon, he looked better. Once again he slept well, ate healthy food, and found the motivation to exercise. His spirits rose and joy began to return to his voice. This woman laid fresh claim on the heart which he thought was lost. And in doing so, she resurrected it from the abyss.

Over the last decade of their marriage, his faith has been reborn. His career has become more than he ever dared to dream. And two beautiful daughters live in a home of peaceful contentment. When love comes, it can change everything, even in the worst of times. Jesus comes to us in love, and my friend ever affirms that it was the love of God that reached him through the tender regard of this woman who saw and still sees something to treasure in a broken man.

This is the kind of love a tax collector named Zacchaeus experienced from Jesus. He is the last recorded person before the passion to begin following Jesus. Zacchaeus, then, is a kind of summary figure of all those whom Jesus had called. The Christ who comes to us in every hour comes also at the last hour to the least likely candidate for discipleship. Zacchaeus is also a last-chance character for us as readers of the gospel. One more person is to be brought in. Even though Zacchaeus was almost too late and nearly got squeezed out by the crowd, Jesus found him. This is a story for all of us, then, who may worry that we blew our chance at living life in healthy, joyful relationship to God. If we think we may have waited too long to get on board with Christ, Zacchaeus tells us it is not too late. The possibility for relationship with God remains open.

We notice immediately that no pity was involved in Zacchaeus' call. He wasn't Christ's charity project. As the woman who fell in love with my friend, Jesus found something desirable in him, before he had changed. Jesus wanted something from one of most detested men in the country. And when Jesus asked to be with him, Zacchaeus changed on the spot. Such love that wants us even as we are, even at the last minute can lead to a rearranging and mending of life that no amount of warnings and condemnations can ever evoke.

His heart slipped through

Zacchaeus' name was a variation on *Zechariah*, which means

"righteous one of God." His name contradicted his life, however, for Zacchaeus was a chief tax collector. He lived in Jericho, a prosperous city that was a gateway to Palestine, situated near a ford in the Jordan River. The robust trade in the town's palm groves and balsam gardens meant a steady flow of commerce along the roads, and thus meant the opportunity for a great deal of tax to be collected. Zacchaeus had become a notoriously wealthy man.

At first thought, we may be surprised as Luke tells us how anxious Zacchaeus was to see Jesus. A man in his position would have insulated himself from those who might make a claim on his well suppressed soul. As I once heard a wealthy miser tragically say, "God can take care of himself; and we'll take care of ourselves." Moreover, Zacchaeus would have hardened himself to the poor he exploited and would not have had much interest in this people's hero. Normally he would not show any enthusiasm for anyone.

So why did he try to see Jesus? What part of his heart slipped up through the protective layers? What desire breached his defenses and seized control of his normally disciplined actions? Zacchaeus, perhaps, had heard that Jesus befriended tax collectors. As we saw in Chapter 3, Levi the publican had actually become one of Jesus' innermost circle of disciples. Though once he might have scoffed at those colleagues who had "got religion," perhaps now his loneliness and years of isolation got the better of him. Perhaps, after all, he had believed what he had been called: traitor, sell-out, unclean. And so hope rose that Jesus might have a new life for him.

But the crowds prevented Zacchaeus from getting a view. He was shorter than most, and I can visualize the people who had suffered under Zacchaeus' extortion relishing a chance to discomfort him. Without a word they closed ranks and blocked him from seeing when Jesus came. It was a momentary victory over this powerful man who happened to be physically small by the socially little who had suffered under him.

The giddy, desperate mood that had seized Zacchaeus, however, would not let him give up. He saw a tree. Then, this shrewd businessman suddenly scrambled up the branches like a child. And there he waited to catch a glimpse of Jesus.

When Jesus reached the spot, though the crowds were clamoring for his attention, he looked up and spotted the tax collector. "Zacchaeus," he called, "Come down immediately. I must stay at your house today" (Luke 19:5). This was more than Zacchaeus could have hoped. Jesus wanted to be with him. He asked Zacchaeus to entertain him. He invited himself to be a social companion of a despised man.

Zacchaeus, of course, came right down and welcomed Jesus gladly. Surely he called for his servants to prepare as quickly as possible the most elaborate feast they could make. He no longer held back his emotions. Beneath the dour, calculating face had been a man longing to be wanted.

The crowd was not pleased with this turn of events. Jesus had chosen the most hated man in the town. Though they should have known by then that this was Jesus' way, they still grumbled, "He has gone to be the guest of a sinner" (19:7). Zacchaeus rushed to Jesus' defense, offering half his possessions to the poor and promising to pay back fourfold any he had defrauded. He was not about to let this moment slip away. He answered the accusations by pouring out his past in a declaration of change. Like Scrooge on Christmas morning, Zacchaeus had discovered beyond hope that it wasn't too late to change, and the joy of it overflowed him.

Today he is at our door

Then Jesus spoke to Zacchaeus what had already become a reality: "Today salvation has come to this house, because this man, too, is a son of Abraham. For the Son of Man came to seek and to save what was lost" (Luke 19:9-10). In the midst of his life as a hated, unwanted, lonely cheat, Jesus had come.

So Jesus comes to us, even when we are years down the wrong road. Even when we have lost our way. Even when we feel thoroughly reprehensible. And he loves us. He regards us and in doing so sees something that he wants. He desires us to host him, to welcome him into our homes and give him what hospitality we have. *Today I must stay at your house.* Such love is not pity but true affection. Somehow, he sees past all the signs that should repel him, into some essential part of us which he loves dearly, desires utterly, no matter how we have marred it.

Perhaps you can hear his voice saying something like this: "Today, I want to stay at your house. I know where you live. I know that you are not ready to host me. There is egg on the coffee table. Dirty clothes are on the bedroom floor. The sheets have not been changed. The windows are filthy. The cheese in the refrigerator is hard and there is no bread. I know all that. But today I must stay at your house. I want to be with you.

"Today, I know your heart. You fear that if you were truly known, you would be surely despised. You feel you must earn love though you are near despair because the competition is so fierce. I know that you hate, that you rage, that you covet. I know that you feel out of control and insatiable in your needs. I know that as surely as I see you in the tree when others have missed you. I know all of who you are as I call you by name.

"And it's all right. I desire to be with you. I long for you to host me in the house of your life. I want you to welcome me with who you are. It's not too late. It's you, yes you, that I want to be with today."

Jesus wants our company. Here is the simple, amazing essence of the gospel. The Son of God has taken on human flesh because he desires to be with us. He wants us to receive him into our hearts and homes. And he comes inviting himself over before we have a chance to prepare anything. Even today. St. John recorded these words of Jesus, "Here I am! I stand at the door and knock. If anyone hears my voice and opens the door, I will come in and eat with him and he with me" (Rev. 3:20). He comes to us when we are not desirable and declares how much he wants to be with us.

He will not be without us

Recently, I got a call from a woman I hadn't heard from in years. We had a teenage romance a quarter century ago, parted friends, but had not kept in touch. She said she wanted to thank me. My interest in her back then came at a time when she was struggling to feel good about herself. Evidently, the time we spent together helped her to grow in many ways. And so she thanked me, all these years later. I was deeply touched by her words, but also knew the truth. I hadn't been on a mission project. I just liked her. I wasn't trying to find someone to help when I spent time with her. I simply enjoyed those wonderful months we were together. She didn't need to thank me for the fact that she was attractive to me. But then as I considered further, I realized the import of what she had said. Isn't the very reality that I wasn't being unselfish and altruistic what made it work? We don't want charity. Even in our loneliness, we want to be wanted for who we are. True love is what sets our hearts singing.

That's the gift Jesus gave to Zacchaeus and offers to us. He has come seeking the lost. He wants to save us. But not merely as an act of divine pity. Jesus came to save us by being fully with us. And as a theologian has said, "God simply *will not* be without us." He truly desires our company. Each one of us has been known since before the foundations of the world were laid. We were uniquely designed for God's pleasure, and he desires to set free in us his joy in our being. Jesus longs to be in continual communion with us.

For this gloriously full salvation he came to us, wedding himself to our humanity. So much does he want to be in our "house" that he literally became bone of our bone and flesh of our flesh. He has taken our condition into himself and so healed it, and us, from within. In Jesus Christ, God has come to be one with us always. Even now, in his glorified life in heaven, he remains fully human as well as fully God. Such news is wonderful beyond hope. He has come to us and he will not leave us; rather he will take us soon to be where he is always.

These were the implications in Jesus' words to Zacchaeus. He restored the man who had once been a tax collector to the original meaning in his name: righteous one of God. For Jesus gave Zacchaeus his own righteousness. Love such as Jesus brings restores us fully. He comes asking us to host him. But when we do open the door, what wonderful hosting gifts he brings! He enters our house and fills it with his peace, his forgiveness, his very being.

Is it any wonder Zacchaeus responded with such joyful abandon? Such love is what sets us free for a new life. The forgiveness implied in his acceptance is what causes true repentance. No matter how far away we have gotten, he knows where to find us. And his words are always for this moment. *Today I must stay at your house.*

Zacchaeus is the last person Luke records as becoming a disciple before Jesus entered his final week, the days leading to his death. Dramatically speaking, Zacchaeus got in just under the wire. Three years of Jesus' ministry had passed. Until nearly the last day, Zacchaeus had been on the outside looking in. I imagine there were many times when he thought he was too far gone to ever turn around and find love and acceptance again. But the meaning of this story is that as long as we live and breathe, it is not too late, not for any of us. Jesus can find us no matter how lost we think we are. He sees us even when we have been forced up a tree. If Zacchaeus can come to Christ, any of us can.

Before turning to the final days of Jesus' time among us, perhaps you might consider if indeed you have heard Jesus knocking at the door of your heart. And if you have heard him, felt him near, have you opened the door? Having worked through twelve chapters about the way Jesus comes to people in every season of life, is this the time to realize that he has truly come to you as well? Even this far down the road of your life, he calls you.

So I invite you before turning another page to come down from the tree and open your house to him. So you may hear the next words spoken as well: Today, salvation has come to this house.

———————————

Dear Jesus, we so long for you to see us, and seeing us to find something you love and desire in us, and loving us to call us to come down and host you. For no matter the years that have passed, the deeds done, or the hardness of heart, we cry out for your forgiving, restoring acceptance. Yes, Lord, come into the house of our hearts. The door is unlocked, we welcome you in. Come into our lives even this moment. Amen.

CHAPTER THIRTEEN

In the Hour of Betrayal
Luke 22:31-32

> *But I have prayed for you, Simon,*
> *that your faith may not fail.*
>
> Luke 22:32

The blind man and Zacchaeus are the last accounts of new disciples following Jesus before his crucifixion. After Jesus' triumphal entry into the city of Jerusalem, the gospel writers concentrate on the events of what has come to be known as Passion Week. We hear Jesus' final teachings to the crowds, many of them warning of a future judgment. These words only intensified his conflict with the religious officials, and the plot against Jesus' life thickened each day. Jesus was keenly aware that the end was approaching, so he gathered his disciples for a final meal and some last words before his death. We have considered throughout this book how Jesus comes to us in every season and hour of life. His days among us were spent in offering his touch, his grace-filled words, his power on behalf of the lost, the sick, the outcast and the forgotten. Jesus came pouring out his life for our sake, and nowhere is this more clearly seen than in the hours before his death.

On the Thursday evening before Good Friday, Jesus gathered with his disciples to celebrate the Passover feast. This was the most sacred meal of the people of Israel. Every year since the Exodus, they gathered as families to remember how God delivered them from slavery in Egypt. Through the ritual of the meal, the stages of their redemption were recounted. The head of the household would lift the cup or offer the bread at the appropriate times, reciting the sacred words that had been handed down through the generations.

Jesus and his disciples had become a family. They were in Jerusalem, far from their homes and relatives in Galilee up north. So, Jesus dined with them in a room of a house that had been rented for the celebration. And he acted as their head, presiding over the Passover. It would be his last meal before crucifixion.

Jesus knew that his time was drawing near. The closer he got to the crucifixion, the more it seems that his awareness sharpened, and his divinity pierced through his humanity. Jesus had sent his disciples to rent the room with these mysterious words, "As you enter the city, a man carrying a jar of water will meet you" (Luke 22:10). How did he know that? There was more, "Follow him to the house that he enters, and say to the owner of the house, 'The Teacher asks: Where is the guest room where I may eat the Passover with my disciples?' He will show you a large upper room, all furnished. Make preparations there" (Luke 22:10-12). There was something divinely appointed about the place. Indeed, the whole scene unfolded with a sense of being scripted ahead of time. There was an air of inevitability. They were entering into sacred time, where the events that occurred were far beyond ordinary. Everything was happening according to a plan.

Yet, as set as the script seemed to be, it was not robotic. Jesus entered the hour freely, and felt the poignancy of his choice. He said, "I have eagerly desired to eat this Passover with you before I suffer" (Luke 22:15). He wanted to be with them, his closest friends, before the terrible hour of his trial. To compare with today, he might have said, "I just wanted to be with you at Christmas, to be together for the best feast, this once, before I've got to go." He felt the sharpness of the moment.

During the rituals of the Passover meal, Jesus wove himself into the sacred rite with words and actions that would reverberate through the centuries. He took the bread, gave thanks, and broke it, and gave it to them, saying, "This is my body given for you. Do this in remembrance of me" (Luke 22:19). Here, in this bread, I am giving myself to you. This bread has already through the years been a sign of your redemption; now see in it as well the giving of my life for you.

Then, Luke tells us in the familiar words, "In the same way, after the supper, he took the cup, saying, 'This cup is the new covenant in my blood, which is poured out for you'" (Luke 22:20). From the faithfulness of God's promises to Israel came a new promise, a new covenant. The cup of redemption lifted at the festive table was filled with the blood of Jesus, poured out for us, to be drunk to the depths for the renewal of our lives.

The giving of this sign of his absolute, complete love for us was, however, interlaced with Jesus' recognition that those whom he loved would soon desert, deny and betray him. Jesus told them, "But the hand of him who is going to betray me is with mine on the table. The Son of Man will go as it has been decreed, but woe to that man who betrays him" (Luke 22:21-22). It is no accident that the words of institution at every Lord's Supper remind us, "On the night in which he was betrayed …" Jesus did not offer us these signs of grace ignorantly. Rather, he looked our human weakness and sin full in the face, and knowing exactly who we are, said "This is my body given for you. This is the eternal promise of my blood offered for you."

The reality they could not see

After the prediction of betrayal, the conversation disintegrated for a time as the disciples "began to question among themselves which of them it might be who would do this" (Luke 22:23). They were horrified to think, there in the afterglow of the celebratory family meal, that they would betray their dear friend and Lord. But their shame turned the focus to themselves. So, very soon the talk devolved to a dispute over which one of them would be considered the greatest. They left Jesus' impending sufferings and concentrated on their own reputations.

Soon after, Jesus turned to Simon Peter and brought them all back to reality. He said, "Simon, Simon, Satan has asked to sift you as wheat. But I have prayed for you, Simon, that your faith may not fail. And when you have turned back, strengthen your brothers" (Luke 22:31-32).

This is a chilling passage. If Jesus' instructions to the disciples about where to find the room for the Passover showed an unveiling of his knowledge about events on the earth, this passage opens a window for us to see Jesus' awareness of the spiritual realm. In his times of prayer, Jesus' knowledge of the Father was so intimate that he could perceive that Satan, the evil one himself, had gone to God making demands concerning the disciples.

Satan had asked to tear them to shreds. The adversary was so audacious that he spoke to God and dared to make demands. He knew that his hour was at hand, when he would get the Son of God delivered to him. Jesus would be given over to his will. And the great destroyer wanted it all. He wanted to sift the disciples until there was nothing left.

The scene was rather pathetic. There were the disciples drinking the wine of the feast and disputing over which one of them was greatest. They were oblivious to how Satan was making ready to crush them. "Simon, Simon," Jesus said, as a parent to a child who has no idea what she's talking about, "Satan, the evil one himself, has asked to have you all." Jesus was patient with them even while he was under the enormous pressure of the hour. He opened their eyes to reality and assured them of how he would protect them.

The intercessions of Jesus

"But I have prayed for you." Interposed between their frail, diluted lives and the rage of the devourer were the prayers of Jesus. Was that enough? Jesus did not promise that he would save his disciples from the time of trial. In fact, he did not pray that the hour of suffering would be removed from them. But he did pray that they would emerge intact from that dreadful night.

The New Testament tells us that the prayers of Jesus have not ceased. Jesus who once prayed in the garden for all the disciples who would come to believe in the future, still prays for us now.

Having joined himself to humanity in the incarnation, the Son of God remains fully human as well as fully God. He has taken our humanity up to heaven. We will discuss this further in Chapter Sixteen, but for now we may consider that Jesus appears before his Father on our behalf. Paul tells us in Romans that "Christ Jesus ... is at the right hand of God and is also interceding for us" (Rom. 8:34). And Hebrews notes that Jesus is our great high priest who "always lives to intercede" for us (Heb. 7:25). So, the intercessions of the man Jesus form a shield around our lives. As with the disciples on that final night, such prayers do not save us from all suffering, attacks of the evil one, or times of trial, but they are able to preserve us through them.

When we follow this story further, we see how the prayers of Christ and the wisdom of God win the hour. In his vicious, insistent demand, Satan had tripped himself up. He asked to sift the disciples like wheat. That is a violent process. The head of the stalk of wheat is smacked and cracked against the threshing floor. Then it is placed in a sieve where it is shaken until all the chaff is separated from the kernels of wheat. The chaff is blown off and scattered to the winds. Only the precious kernels remain. Perhaps Satan only looked at the metaphor partially – he thought of the sifting process. Perhaps he thought the disciples were all chaff anyway, so weak and frail that nothing would be left. There would be no kernels worth saving. All would be blown away. But that did not happen. Seeds of faith that would grow to transform history endured through the sifting.

As ever, the plan of God takes what is worthless and makes it of infinite value. He takes what is failed and makes it the pillar of success. He takes what is weak and makes it strong. What is discarded becomes a jewel of great price.

Simon Peter was indeed sifted like wheat. His three denials of knowing Jesus stabbed him to the quick. But the intercessions of Jesus preserved the kernel of his faith, his soul, through the trial. After the resurrection, Jesus healed Peter. He asked him in front of the others to his declare his devotion. Simon Peter replied earnestly, "Yes, Lord, you know that I love you" (John 21:15). Then Jesus asked him a second time and a third, until Peter had confessed his love publicly as many times as he had denied his Lord. And each time Jesus reminded Peter of the task he had given him in the Upper Room. "Feed my sheep" (John 21:17), he told Peter, echoing the command that flowed from his prayers, "And when you have turned back, strengthen your brothers." Simon Peter became the fearless leader of the newly borning church, the brave proclaimer of the resurrection. The prayers of Jesus were effective.

What once separated us now unites us

In the hour of our betrayal, Christ comes to us. God does not flee when we deny him. Even in the midst of our heinous sin and embarrassing failures, Christ is praying for us. He appears before his Father on our behalf, and makes intercession for us. And through Christ, the Father is weaving all things together for good "for those who love him, who have been called according to his purpose" (Rom. 8:28).

The story of the Lord's Supper shows us how Jesus can take the very things that divide us from him and use them to bind us to himself. In our church membership classes, we invite people to draw a timeline of their relationship with God. I have been impressed with how many mark the times of trial as the occasions for the most significant growth. Our very suffering can lead us into a depth of communion with God that many say is worth every bit of the cost. From our mistakes and our weakness, God makes more than we could ever have dared to hope.

For example, sometimes we flee from him, choosing everything but God. We squander our health, our time, our money. We dive into the world, and pursue fulfillment down every wrong path. But God does not cut us off in disgust. When we have run our course, we wake up, as the prodigal son did, in the pig sty, far from home, broke and hungry in the midst of a famine. There we discover that our very flight from God has become the yearning to go home. And he is there, waiting with open arms, rushing to welcome us back into the embrace of love. Christ uses our rebellion to awaken our deepest longing for him.

Consider as well how some of us bear a searing sense of

humiliation for what has been done to us. We have believed that the abuse we have taken must somehow have been our fault. We must have asked for it, or deserved it. And we live embarrassed by what has happened, by who has left us and how blind we were to what was coming. But the story of the Last Supper urges us to look at Jesus most especially when we are feeling isolated by shame.

Jesus' closest friends all ran away in his time of trial. His intimate companion sold him to his enemies for a bag of silver. His sworn defender let a servant maid intimidate him into denying his Lord. The Son of God went alone to the trial. He was mocked and humiliated. Yet, on the night of his betrayal, he gave us the bread and cup. So when we go to him with our shame and embarrassment we find a communion in humiliation with him. We drink the cup and find our loss mingled with his, and we are transformed. Jesus knew the raw shame of human abuse, and he gave himself to us in the midst of it. Thus we may find our suffering taken up in his and healed.

But what of those who have done things so horrible that we could never forgive? How does Jesus take those awful sins and turn them into a sign of our union with him? Think of his passion, which followed the supper. Is Christ's love for everyone? Consider that when the light of the glory of God shone in the face of Jesus, revealing the loving Father, we humans backhanded that face with the hard glove of a Roman soldier. The mouth of Jesus spoke words of grace to set the guilty free, and we, we the human race, shouted him silent with cries of "Crucify, crucify!" The hands of Jesus healed the sick, and we humans took those hands and drove iron spikes through them. The back of Jesus bore the weight of the world and we gave it 39 lashes before making him slide his open flesh against the rough splinters of the cross. And nevertheless Jesus, on the night of his betrayal, said "This is my body, broken for you. For you. For you. This is my blood poured out for the forgiveness of sins, even the sins committed against me."

Faced with such love, we realize ever more clearly what we have done. When we know our sin in such raw recognition, we cry out for a savior. And we find one. In his wisdom, God takes what separates us from him, even in horror and shame, and uses that very thing to bind us to himself.

No one can outscheme the love of God. Satan got what he asked for and sifted Peter and the disciples. And Satan lost. They came through. Their betrayal and denial became the words of the sign at the heart of the universe: God gives himself utterly to us in Christ Jesus. Even in the hour before we handed him over to be tried and crucified, Christ offered himself to us. So we may take and eat, take and drink and receive completely what he gives.

Our very shame, our very failure, our very sin that caused the shame and ruin of the cross has been used by God for redeeming the world. "Simon, Simon, Satan has asked to sift you as wheat. But I have prayed for you." Against all the powers of destruction in the universe, those six words stand triumphant. Jesus says, "But I have prayed for you." He prays for us even now. And it is enough.

Lord Jesus, pray for us. For we are tossed with doubt and torn apart with fears. Before we know it, we deny you. In a moment, we would desert you. We pray now amazed at your prayers for us. Knowing who we are, still you give yourself to us. You take the very signs that remind us of our betrayal and make them the signs of how you bind yourself to us forever. Lord Jesus, pray for us, oh do not cease! And we will be sustained. Amen.

CHAPTER FOURTEEN

Words from the Cross
Luke 23:26-43

*Father, forgive them, for they
do not know what they are doing.*

Luke 23:34

The night of Jesus' betrayal became a midnight trial and a sentence of death at dawn. In this chapter, we will go with Jesus to the cross. And we will see that even there he gave himself in love on our behalf. In the midst of physical agony, Jesus nevertheless turned his loving attention to the people nearby. On the cross, his focus was still outward. While his strength was being drained by our violence, he yet poured out the little life he had left in words of grace. The cross becomes the ultimate sign of how Christ comes to us in every season of life. It gives weight and substance to the words, "I am with you always."

We have recorded in Luke's gospel words Jesus spoke on the way to crucifixion, as well as three of his seven sentences from the cross. Jesus was weak from the flogging ordered by the Roman governor, Pilate. So the soldiers seized Simon of Cyrene, a bystander, to carry the cross for him. As they made their way through the streets of Jerusalem, from Pilate's palace to the garbage dump and killing field known as the Skull, a crowd followed along. Among them were women who mourned and wailed for Jesus.

Jesus turned to these women and said, "Daughters of

Jerusalem, do not weep for me; weep for yourselves and for your children. For the time will come when you will say, 'Blessed are the barren women, the wombs that never bore and the breasts that never nursed!'" (Luke 23:28-29).

Do not weep for me; weep for yourselves and for your children. Moments before the excruciating torture of a Roman cross, Jesus looked at those who wept and thought not of himself but of them. Jesus spoke right to their very identity as women. These daughters of first century Israel had been reared to know that the sacred joy of womanhood is the bearing of children. To miss this joy was to be cursed, and the barren were considered afflicted. What could possibly make a woman wish she had not nursed the beloved babe upon her breast?

Only the intolerable situations of life, when it seems that enduring in this world is more than anyone can bear. And such would be the case for those who rejected the Son of God, not recognizing who had come among them. Such would be the case for God's people when, trying yet again to bring in the kingdom through a political solution, they provoked Rome to react. In A.D. 70, the Roman army swept through Jerusalem, destroying the temple and scattering the people. Such is the case more often in this life than we may realize. Going to the cross, Jesus knew his own people had to endure cross-like situations.

Suspended on the beams

Once I spoke with a man who was watching his marriage come to an end. It was not what he wanted and not at all what he had expected. She was gone. She had a phone number he couldn't get and if he called at work, she wouldn't talk. She was looking to someone else for support and intimacy. At the deepest level, he just couldn't find her anymore.

But neither could he let her go. "This is my wife," he said. "We took vows before all our friends and family. This is for life. I didn't take those vows lightly." He loved her still. She bore his name. But she had gone. And the more he sought her, the further removed she got. It was killing him, physically as well as spiritually.

As I looked at him, I felt so viscerally, "You're on the cross. I feel you suspended on the beams. You can go neither forward nor back. You just have to endure this hell that has no solution."

I didn't expect that my words would be of much comfort in the moment, but hoped the connection would return to mind some time in the future. I spoke some halting lines which I hoped he would hear like this: "I think you're where Jesus was. He came to love us. He had a legitimate claim on us. He is our creator and he called us to himself. But we fled him. He could not force us and have us be free. On the cross he was suspended in agony by his love. Rejected by us, he nevertheless could not let us go. So he endured in love until it killed him. I know that may not help much now, but at least you know you have some company in this feeling."

Daughters of Jerusalem, do not weep for me, but for your-selves and for your children. Jesus knew that living in a world such as this, there would be times when we would have to join him on the cross. Those who love inevitably find that there are hours when we can go neither forward nor backward, but must wait helplessly for the other to determine our fate.

Parents may feel suspended on the cross when their children pass through adolescence. We rear our children with all the love and skill we have, then must in due course let them go to make their own way. And though our hearts break, we cannot but watch them as they stumble into the pain of mistakes that will make them men and women. How excruciating is the watching! They are our flesh and blood. We held them so long under the roof of our homes and hearts. We would gladly give our lives on their behalf. They bear our name and our genes. We have a claim of love on them. Yet to speak may drive them away. To rescue them may drive them deeper into danger. To offer advice may elicit the exact opposite result. How many mothers and fathers yearn after their children while they feel hung on the beams of love, unable to go forward or back? We endure the years of rejection, the agony of the damage done, the pain of wrong choices all the while praying for the days of resurrection to come.

These feelings of being stretched and suspended in an agony

of love may occur for every sensitive heart that looks upon the world and believes it was meant to be more. We know that things are not as they should be. Something better was intended and will come to be when the kingdom of God is at last fulfilled. But now, in the meantime, we are in the pain of the interim. Whatever form our particular burdens take, the dynamic is the same. Whether we ache as we walk the hallways littered with declining bodies now devoid of coherent minds or cry as we see the earth pillaged and pocked from our greed, whether our hearts break over what is done to the children or feel the confusion of a culture that grows noisier by the second, we know that life is meant to be different. Sometimes we wonder if it would be better if no more children were born into a world such as this. Daughters of Jerusalem, weep not for me but for yourselves. Jesus knows.

Father, forgive them

Then, from his position of hanging in the excruciating conflict between his love for us and our rejection of him, Jesus prayed, "Father, forgive them, for they do not know what they are doing" (Luke 23:34). That Jesus prayed for our forgiveness does not surprise me. He came to give his life for us, to create a new and living way to God. But that second line worries me, "they do not know what they are doing." Is that some kind of mitigating circumstance? Is the basis for our forgiveness the fact that we were ignorant of who we put to death?

I believe that even knowing what we did, we would have done it anyway. I hear the crowd described in Matthew's account taking feverish responsibility for Pilate's judgment, "Let his blood be on us and on our children!" (Matt. 27:25). To me, we knew enough. We human beings knew that here was the light of the world and we wanted to be left alone in the darkness. We wanted to snuff out that light.

But surely Jesus knew that. He, after all, had predicted the betrayal and denial of his intimate friends. Perhaps he means that we neither know the true depth of our sin nor the true extent of God's love. However much we might know of who Christ is, our capacity to reject him in sin would be there. But never will we

fully understand the depth of his love for us. Knowing the lostness in us more than we will ever grasp, still God did not spare
his own Son but freely gave him up for us. There is in Christ on
the cross revealed a love of God beyond measurement of height
and depth. And in his words of forgiveness from the cross, he
comes to us with the great secret of how we may endure the harm
that is done to us.

A man in his nineties, of keen mind and rich soul, was told
he needed surgery to clear the carotid artery in his neck. To
decline the procedure would be to live with a high risk of a debilitating stroke. Yet to have the surgery also incurred risks as well.
Unafraid of death and full of courage, he went to the hospital.
The artery was successfully cleared, but during the process, a bit
of plaque broke off and caused the very stroke he had hoped to
prevent.

Suddenly, this gracious man who loved to talk with others
found himself on the cross. He was suspended between knowing
what he wanted to say and being unable to say it. This situation
was in some ways worse than death. He was here in this world yet
unable to be in it as a communicator.

The surgeon came into his room to explain what had happened. The young doctor apologized profoundly that the procedure had caused such an impairment. The elderly man, who had
been able to say only a few words, worked furiously to get something out. Finally, it came. He made a sweeping motion with arms
and said clearly, "Mistakes happen." He forgave. From the position of a cross, the true essence of Christian personality came
out. Mistakes happen. I don't hold it against you. Though I am in
the agony of being unable to speak, I will not put that burden on
you. Instead, I will release you, and begin the long road of work
back to speech.

And beyond expectations, his speech is returning. It is heard
most clearly in moments such as when he reached up his hand to
the night nurse's cheek and told her, "You are a very good
woman." Or when he directs the attention of the conversation to
those who have come to see him. This is the spirit of Christ on
the cross, who turned out from his agony in prayers of forgive-

ness. Because Christ came to us praying our grace in that hour, he has opened this way of loving kindness to those who come after.

Today you will be with me in paradise

On either side of Jesus, two thieves were also crucified. One mocked Jesus, saying sarcastically, "Aren't you the Christ? Save yourself and us!" (Luke 23:39). But the thief on the other cross rebuked the scoffer. He had accepted that he was receiving nothing less than he deserved. Then he pleaded to Jesus for mercy, "Jesus remember me when you come into your kingdom" (Luke 23:42). Quite a faith is revealed when we remember that the thief was asking for mercy from a man who would die before he did! And from the cross, Jesus blessed the man with a promise, "... today you will be with me in paradise" (Luke 23:43). Even in the hours of his dying, Jesus was seeking and saving the lost. And this scene tells us that even in the worst of times, a blessing may come.

The week I worked on this passage for a Sunday sermon, our entire congregation unexpectedly went on the cross with a young family. Their three-year-old son choked while eating a hot dog. The parents couldn't dislodge it. They phoned the emergency medical team and sought neighbors' help. But the little boy was soon unconscious. What do you do when you do all you can and it doesn't work? How can you live when you want to give all you have but have no way to make it count? How does one endure such a cross?

The word spread through the church like a brush fire. People wept and prayed. The young boy was being rushed to the hospital. As I jumped in my car, I knew how far it was from their house to the emergency room. Not nearly close enough for a boy who wasn't breathing. I tried to think of what I would say to parents who had seen their child die in their arms. I prayed and I bargained with God, knowing full well that these situations rarely work out the way we hope.

God granted miracles in three waves. First, the boy arrived at the hospital alive. The family paced the halls, with their souls on a cross. The medical team worked and people kept praying. Nearly losing him again, the doctors finally got the obstruction from lungs and throat. But would he ever be himself again? The signs weren't good. He was airlifted to a larger hospital, and a few hours later, the second miracle came. His brain appeared undamaged. But his lungs had not fared so well. The next morning's x-ray predicted a long stay on a ventilator and potentially permanent damage. But then, by four that afternoon, his lungs were clear – a third miracle.

The next Sunday, the young man was in his mother's arms in the Palm Sunday procession, and the congregation wept openly. Easter had come early. No matter our faith, things don't have to work out that way. We were let off the beams of our helplessness in a sweet, rare victory for light and life. All glory be to God!

For us, Jesus words came from the cross, as they did to the thief next to him, "Today you will be with me in Paradise." He speaks from the place of agony and offers hope. Though the thief would die along with Jesus, he learned that his suffering would not be meaningless. It would lead to everlasting life. That terrible week, in the midst of suffering came the breath of heaven to a family and a foretaste to all of us that there is glory and life to come. Though we will not get every miracle we ask for, this one encouraged us with the presence of God and assured us that indeed God is making something redemptive out of our suffering.

The touch of God in the cross

Even from the cross Jesus gave himself to us. His presence there can make all the difference in the trials we undergo. In a touchingly pastoral sermon, Thomas Torrance has written:

> It is the same God who delivered up his Son for us on the Cross who will continue to care for us day by day, no matter what happens. The very same Love of God is able, now, and every day, to make everything work together for good – and he does it through the Cross, his divine sacrifice. The Cross means that God does not hold himself aloof from us. And so whatever may befall us, in grief or pain, or loss, we may take it to Calvary and let it feel the touch of God in the

Cross, where the infinite sacrifice of the Father and of the Son are forever inseparably bound together.

Because the cross of Christ's agony is a gift to us, we may go there with our sorrows and pain. We bring our situations to the cross and let them feel the touch of God in the cross. When we find a connection point between the terrible, suspending pain of our trials and the cross of Christ, we see there God's touch. He takes our pain unto himself and tends it. He can redeem the situations of our lives so that, beyond hope, something good can come even of the worst situation.

George Herbert understood this when, in a poem called "Affliction (3)," he prayed to Jesus:

> *"Thy life on earth was grief, and thou art still*
> *Constant unto it."*

Jesus the man of sorrows lived and died in the affliction of humanity. He is intimately acquainted with all our pains. But hear the news: he is still constant unto the grief. He still attends to the grief of this mortal life.

This Christ still lives in us through his Spirit, and together we are his body. He makes his appeal to the world through us. Though he suffered once for all on the cross, he continues to pray for us in heaven. There, still fully human as well as fully God, he experiences, as in his own body, the joys and sufferings of his people. We have a mystical link with him. In affliction, we enter what Paul has described as "the fellowship of his sufferings" (Phil. 3:10). Herbert says that Christ is

> *"making it to be*
> *A point of honor, now to grieve in me,*
> *And in thy members suffer ill."*

As we are afflicted, Christ shares in the grief. He grieves in us. In his people, he suffers their ills.

Even on the cross, Christ turned out from himself and toward us in forgiveness. He opened the way for us to come to him on the cross with our pains and sorrows. Bringing the suffering one our suffering, we see in the cross the touch of God. And that touch is soothing. That presence is healing. Though our circumstances may not change we see our lives taken up in Christ, even our griefs taken into his grief, and we are not alone. Moreover, we have the confidence that God will work even our grief for the good, making us more and more like his Son and fitting us for eternal life.

Father, into your hands

Finally, we hear Jesus cry out, "Father, into your hands I commit my spirit" (Luke 23:46). Matthew and Mark both record that before this final utterance, Jesus knew a moment of forsakenness on the cross. Though a very little time in our world, the agony of that separation was for Jesus an eternity of loss. Cut off from the consciousness of his Father's presence, the Son of God who has from all eternity existed in unbroken fellowship with the Father experienced utter abandonment. Christ underwent the pains of hell for us on the cross. The great theologians of the Church have all been stunned by this moment. As Doug Kelly has said, "In that moment the Father turned his favorable gaze from the face of his ever beloved Son who had become the vilest of sin. These moments of divine agony far outweigh the pain of eternal hell a finite person would feel." Martin Luther asked, "How can it be, God forsaken by God?" And Calvin commented, "Never did the Father love his Son more than in these moments when he spent himself in love for us." Never did the Father grieve more over the sin of the world than when his own heart broke at the agony endured by the Son.

And then Jesus committed himself into his Father's hands. Had the forsakenness passed, and did Jesus having tasted hell then enter confidently into the release of physical death? Or, still feeling forsaken by his Father, did he nevertheless give himself in sheer, naked faith to the Father he could not sense but believed was there? We cannot know. We stand in the place where our mouths must be shut in wonder. We simply behold the utter faithfulness and the absolute pouring out of body and soul of one on behalf of another. On behalf of us.

In the dark, disturbing days, we taste a bit of the agony of love. We feel what it is to be suspended between unbearable options, unable to go forward or back. This suffering cannot be removed. It is our lot. But we may in the midst of it enter the fellowship of his sufferings. We may go and touch the cross and feel the touch of God in it. In the cross our sins are forgiven. All our griefs are borne, and Jesus is still constant unto them. In the cross is the offering of God on our behalf. And you and I are not alone. Jesus is still giving himself to us. He is still making something glorious out of the suffering and pain of this life. In this moment, feel the touch of God in the cross and your sufferings and sins placed there.

*F*ather, how could you forgive us for putting to death your Son? Yet nowhere do we see your love more clearly than on the cross. Having every claim on us, you would not force your will upon us. Rather, Christ let his loving hands be suspended on the rough beams of the cross. Knowing the agony that is part of human life and love, Jesus comes to us with the power of his sacrifice. You feel what we feel, and you can make something good arise from it. Thank you for taking up our suffering as well as our sin and enfolding both in your love. Amen.

CHAPTER FIFTEEN

In the Turning of the Tears

John 20:10-18

... she turned around and saw Jesus ...

John 20:14

The resurrection of Jesus is a singularity, an unrepeatable event that occurred once in the realm of earth and swiftly passing time in which we live. It was an historical occurrence. A dead man got up. Jesus' resurrection is the irreducible, central event of Christianity. It is the great fact around which all other truths now revolve, and it is the best possible news for the human race. Through the ages, the people of Christ have always confessed that Jesus rose bodily from the dead. Without a real resurrection, as Paul writes, our "faith is futile; you are still in your sins ... those who have fallen asleep in Christ are lost. If only for this life we have hope in Christ, we are to be pitied more than all men" (I Cor. 15:17-19). If the Jesus who was crucified did not truly rise, then the whole premise that Christ comes to us in every hour is mere sentiment. But, as Paul continues, "Christ has indeed been raised from the dead" (I Cor. 15:20) and so our hope is boundless. There is real substance behind Christ's words, "I am with you always."

Of course, because the resurrection is a singularity, it is difficult to believe. This news demands that all our thinking about the way life and the world work be revised. For Jesus' rising does not fit the worldview of our current Western culture, and even the most ardent Christians will struggle with doubt. We need connection points with that which necessarily always remains above our ability to measure, prove, analyze and manage it. While the resurrection is beyond our grasp, its truth and power are not beyond our experience. We may indeed find ways into the meaning of this event for present daily life that will then go on to assure us of its significance for our life beyond this world in the future. I have often found that even very small portions of the gospel accounts of the resurrection contain potent measures of meaning for us. So in this chapter, let us consider how Jesus comes to us in his rising by examining three parts of the story as recorded in John 20.

Looking into the tomb

At the earliest possible moment, Mary Magdalene had gone to the tomb to care for the body of Jesus. She found the stone rolled away from the cave. The body was not inside. Immediately she ran to find Simon Peter and John. Breathlessly she told them, "They have taken the Lord out of the tomb, and we don't know where they have put him" (John 20:2). To Mary, this was the final insult. Wasn't it enough that they had beaten him, mocked him, and killed him? Did they have to desecrate his grave as well? Would there be no opportunity for her to pour her grief over his bruised, dead body?

When Peter and John heard her story, they ran with her back to the tomb. They wanted to see what had happened, though of course their haste would make no difference. John was the faster. He got there first, but did not go in. He only bent down, peered inside, and saw the linen cloths that had wrapped Jesus' body lying there, with nothing inside them. Then Peter came, and with his usual impetuosity, plunged into the tomb. He saw the burial strips lying there and the cloth that had been on Jesus' head. The headpiece was not with the other garments. It was rolled up in a place by itself.

Then John went in. And the text tells us "He saw and believed" (John 20:8). But what did he believe? That the body of

Jesus had been stolen? The graveclothes were too neatly arranged to indicate robbery. No thief would carefully roll up the head cloth. What did John believe?

Our text adds, "They still did not understand from Scripture, that Jesus had to rise from the dead. Then the disciples went back to their homes" (John 20:9-10). John believed – something – but did not understand the full implications of what he believed. Overwhelmed, he returned to the place where a more ordinary life of grief had been unfolding. We are presented with two statements, then, that don't fit very well together. *He saw and believed ... They still did not understand.* For the next hours of that first Easter Day, the disciples would be suspended between the wild intuitions of the heart and the incomprehension of the mind. Jesus was gone from the tomb. Could it be? Could he be alive? Such news seemed good beyond belief.

They came to gaze inside a tomb. All the signs of death were there, except a body. The trappings of finality presented themselves: the stone, the graveclothes, the spices, and the blood. It looked like death. Mary and the women mentioned in the other Gospels had come to pay attention to death. They came to tend a corpse in loving memory. But looking closely, they discovered that there was no body. Jesus was not in the tomb.

We may find here a metaphor for our lives. I suspect many of us know what it is to have a tomb located in a garden in our lives, filled with all the accoutrements of death. We go there to pay homage on a regular basis, and expect the grave to be occupied.

For instance, in the midst of a happy, ordered life, there may be the anger you have nursed into an enduring grudge. Once you were wronged. Deeply. By someone who never asked for forgiveness. This one seemed rather pleased to have hurt you, or at best so blindly unaware of your feelings that no harm could have been imagined. Your hurt was intense. A part of you died at the hands of the one who harmed you.

And so you found a tomb for the dead part, tucked away in a quiet garden of pleasant appearances. There you have gone night after night, in secret, to tend the dead body. You have pored over that hurt until it became anger and the rage grew like the living dead. It sank roots of bitterness. It grew into the thorny briar of a perennial hatred.

In the daylight world, everyone may know you as a kind and loving person. You bring food to others in need, remember the appropriate phone calls, make the usual inquiries. But few know the location of your secret tomb where you pay a daily visit to something long dead and rotting.

The story of the first Easter morning, though, creates a shocking twist to the routine. You go to your tomb of bitterness and find the cave disturbed. The stone has been rolled away. Someone has been tampering with your private garden! You have been found out! You go over to feel the graveclothes. All the form is there. The shape of the arguments and the hurts. But there is no substance. The body has vanished. Only air is inside the cloths. The stench of the old wounds has vanished and the cave is freshening in the sunlight that pours through the long-sealed entrance. You see but do not understand. You believe that the corpse is gone but do not yet know how to deal with the possibility of freedom and new life. Perhaps like Peter and John, you want to run back to the comfort of the ordinary until you can make sense of this change.

What has happened? The resurrection of Jesus has burst the tombs of bitterness and deathly grudges. Dying, Jesus absorbed the rage of the world into himself. Sin became his, both our sin and the sins committed against us. He took their pain and all the resulting anger. The weight of the world piled him down into the tomb. But rising, Jesus cast aside death, sin and rage even as he threw off the graveclothes. They were no longer necessary for him, and now, in Christ, they are not necessary to us.

The heart may leap at such a possibility. Might I really be free from all the dark caves? Could it be that as he rises Christ takes me by the hand and raises me, too? It is beyond our minds' ability to grasp how this transfer can be. We cannot follow the connections that allow one man to take the sins of many nor fathom the power that declares, "For as in Adam all die, so in Christ all will be made alive" (I Cor. 15:22). Jesus is risen and he has taken even our anger up in the joy of his forgiveness. It's gone. So we may let go of these grave trappings and get on with a life of love. Christ took our hurt with him in his death. And he has taken our anger away with him in his rising. Hearing this amazing story may be for us similar to the disciples' looking at the empty strips of linen. We see and believe but do not yet understand all this means.

Mary

Overwhelmed with the implications of what they saw, John and Peter left the tomb to sort things out back in town. But Mary stayed in the garden and continued to cry. Hers is the most poignant of all the resurrection stories. Mary had come to the tomb to anoint the body of Jesus with spices that would preserve it. She hoped to complete the burial rites they had begun Friday evening shortly before the Sabbath had interrupted them. And she wanted the chance to hold him one more time. After the horror of Friday, she wanted to see him at peace now. Mary loved Jesus yet, and in the distorted lengthening of the hours that often follows a death, it was only the thought of seeing him again that got her through.

And so the sight that greeted her was all the more bewildering. The body was gone. Mary thought the authorities had stolen it. As if crucifixion were not sufficient, now they would not allow the body of Jesus to be at rest. And so Mary was not allowed any finality in her grief. Seeing the empty tomb, her weeping was all the more. Her good grieving had been suspended. For it found no location, no body on which to alight. This tragedy never ended. They were still doing things to him.

Then two angels inside the cave asked her, "Woman, why are you crying?" (John 20:13). Mary, apparently so focused on loss that she was undaunted by the angelic presence, answered, "They have taken my Lord away and I don't know where they have put him" (John 20:13). She speaks of him as if his dead body were her Jesus, so diminished were her expectations at the tomb. The body, the corpse would be enough for her, if only they had not taken it.

Then Mary turned around and saw Jesus. She did not recognize him. Mary supposed him to be the gardener. Perhaps he would know where the body had been taken. Grief found its voice in insistence, "Sir, if you have carried him away, tell me where you have put him, and I will get him" (John 20:15). She was saying in effect, "Do not deny me any longer; you don't even need to help me; just show the way and I will get him."

And then there came the turning of the tears.

Jesus spoke to her one word, "Mary."

The steady rain of her tears had blocked all sight of the world beyond the windows of her eyes. Now the rains ceased and the waters parted. *Mary!*

She saw that it was the Lord. "Rabboni! My teacher!" She fell at his feet and held on to him hard. He was alive. How could it be? His voice still sounded in her mind, the voice like no other. *Mary*. She knew then. Peter and John had believed without understanding, but now Mary grasped the full truth that Jesus was alive again. And the rain of tears fell once more, though now she was weeping for joy. It was the turning of the tears.

Will Mary's story provide us with a connection point to the resurrection of Jesus?

'The darkling drag'

At the beginning of a poem by Robert Penn Warren, a man and a woman are swimming in the Pacific Ocean at dusk. Stars begin to appear in the gloaming sky above them. They look up at the starlight, drawn toward eternity, even as they feel underneath them the depths of the ocean tugging them downward. Eternity pulling from above, oblivion from below, and the man and the woman swimming in between.

That couple is every one of us, swimming through our brief days in the world. Eternity is set in our hearts; we look toward the stars, but perilous waters could wash over us and drag us down at any moment. As they swim side by side, Warren writes that

> *"... they feel the sea's long swell*
> *And the darkling drag of nameless depth below."¹*

The darkling drag of nameless depth below. Perhaps not all those depths are nameless. I think sometimes that I have heard their names spoken in tears.

We have already considered the tug of ancient anger in our lives. There is as well the darkling drag of fear which pulls in a long slow swell beneath us. The midnight questions come: Will everything be all right? Will I be able to do what I need to do before time or illness stops me? Will I be found out and have the hollow inside of my shining life exposed? We may be stricken with fears that we will never find or fulfill God's plan for us. We worry that people could never love us if they truly knew us. And always, always, time presses against us with the urgency of its passing amidst the frightening uncertainty of what lies ahead.

All these fears are well grounded. For life is dangerous. The world is unfriendly. We are frail. We indeed may not be able to protect that which we love. We very well may *not* succeed at the tasks to which we are called. The whole thing at any moment really could collapse in a heap at our feet. The truth that drives our fears is enough to make us cry out.

Perhaps we find ourselves standing by the tomb where our fears have been realized, hoping only to tend the corpse left behind by vanished dreams. And then Jesus comes to us risen from the grave. He arrives from a time of having the deepest fear of every human soul come to pass: being utterly alone, betrayed and completely shamed, abandoned even by God. Up from that hell, Jesus comes, and he speaks. He utters one word to each of us. Jesus calls your name and mine.

And for us as for Mary there comes the turning of the tears. He calls us by name and suddenly everything falls into place. We are not alone. God knows us and calls us by name. He loves us. He will not let us go. Jesus has been swept under by the darkling drag of our fears and returned with news of great peace. All is well. God's love has reached beneath the depths of our lostness and lifted us up, back into the light of his presence. The future we so fear belongs to the loving God.

There are people in the worst of circumstances who will bear witness to this truth. I have seen courage in the face of insurmountable obstacles and the tenacious will of love that will not let the beloved go. Even more, I have felt the peace that passes understanding. Deeper than the darkling depths of our worst fears, this peace assures us that everything is all right. Sometimes, just when we feel completely helpless and out of control, there comes the confidence that we are loved. We are kept and held. Even facing a terrible future, people have known with certainty that God exists and is holding all things together for good. Such courage sees beyond present appearances. Even with all present evidence to the contrary, it grasps the future God has secured for us.

Everything in the short term might still turn out terribly. Life remains perilous. But there are some who have known that in spite of everything, right now, it is all right. Jesus has risen from the dead. Life will conquer death; righteousness will one day replace injustice; joy will triumph over despair. From a source unknown to us before comes the courage of resurrection. Jesus comes to us and turns the tears of fear to peace. And so we may declare along with Mary, "I have seen the Lord!" (John 20:18).

Thomas

That same night, Jesus appeared to the other disciples in the upper room. He showed them his pierced hands and side, and declared "Peace be with you!" (John 20:19). He breathed on them the promise of the Holy Spirit and charged them to go into the world, sent as he had been sent. By then the disciples not only believed but understood that Jesus was truly risen.

Except for Thomas. For some reason, he had not been in the room with the others. They blurted out the reason for their joy to him just as Mary had, "We have seen the Lord!" (John 20:25). But despite the empty tomb and their eyewitness accounts, Thomas just couldn't believe it. Resurrection did not fit either his expectations or his worldview. He was a realist, and life does not return to those who have died. Thomas told them, "Unless I see the nail marks in his hands and put my finger where the nails were and put my hand into his side, I will not believe it" (John 20:25). He wanted more than a story; Thomas demanded personal experience and sensory evidence.

We may be thankful for Thomas' doubts. For he is our man on the scene. Thomas represents all of us who were not there when the risen Jesus appeared. He speaks for us when he voices his concern that these kinds of things just don't happen. For all of us who feel we missed the one class when the keys to understanding were passed out, Thomas is our man. Others may have been gifted with easy faith, but we have always struggled. We want to know with certainty and there seems little to be had. Go on Thomas, and make your demands for all of us!

Thomas did get what he asked for. A week later Jesus came to his disciples again and this time Thomas was with them. Jesus spoke to him, "Put your finger here; see my hands. Reach out your hand and put it into my side. Stop doubting and believe" (John 20:27). Jesus showed Thomas the pierced hands of a real body, once dead but now risen. He offered him a touch of the side pierced by the wound of love. Concrete evidence was at hand.

And curiously, the account does not tell us whether Thomas actually touched Jesus or not. Rather, right after Jesus' offer, we hear Thomas declare, "My Lord and my God!" (John 20:28). Perhaps he did touch Jesus, or perhaps none of that made any difference. Jesus had come to him in risen glory and offered himself. He exhorted Thomas to put away his doubt and start believing. That was enough for Thomas. Interestingly, the biggest doubter, the last holdout, ended up being the one who made the strongest declaration of who Jesus is in all the gospels! *"My Lord and my God!"* This skeptic became the boldest confessor.

Then Jesus spoke further to Thomas, though it seems he had us in mind as well, "Because you have seen me, you have believed; blessed are those who have not seen and yet have believed" (John 20:29). Thomas received the visit from the risen Christ that he demanded and it was sufficient to kindle his faith. Jesus ascended to heaven forty days after the resurrection, and thus his risen body is now beyond human perception. Very few of us, no matter our demands, will have even a visionary experience of Christ. We are those who are called to believe though we do not see. Nearly two thousand years ago, Jesus shot his words toward all believers in the future, and blessed us in the difficulty of this demand. Is that enough for those who are skeptical?

If you are one who continues to find the resurrection difficult to embrace but long to do so, I hope you will find Thomas to be your friend and advocate. I wonder if you could attach yourself to him. Be with him in his disappointment at missing the first visit from Jesus. Feel your need for concrete evidence in his demands for proof. And then ask yourself how you would respond if indeed you could see the nailprints in the hands of Christ. What would you do if Jesus asked you to touch that wounded side from which the blood that cleansed the world of sin once flowed?

We all need to turn a sharp eye on the doubts we have. Too often we can let our struggles with unanswerable questions provide cover for us so that we do not have to deal with the Christ who comes and calls us to himself. So we each have to ask, "Would I throw my doubts up even if they were all answered? Or am I ready and waiting for Christ to make himself known to me? Am I anxious to join doubting Thomas as the boldest believer and cry out to Jesus, "My Lord and my God!"

If we earnestly desire Christ to make himself real to us in his resurrection power, I believe that he will do that. Yes, the event of his rising is a singularity and as such it asks to reshape the way we think about God, life, death and the world. The resurrection is so hugely significant that it threatens to overwhelm us and we struggle with believing for good reason. But though we may not now see the risen Jesus in the flesh, we may experience the truth and power of his rising. People today are still finding the grave-clothes of their old wounds empty. Fresh air and dawn light still flood the ancient tombs. The darkling drag of fear, guilt and loss may threaten to pull us under. But in this very hour, there are those whose tears are being turned.

At the end of John 20, the author turns to the readers and reminds us of why he recorded these signs and stories of Jesus: "These are written that you may believe that Jesus is the Christ, the Son of God, and that by believing you may have life in his name" (John 20:31). Thomas stayed with the company of the believing disciples even when he could not believe. He kept close to the place where Jesus was known to have shown up. We, too, may go to the fellowship of Christ's people and to the stories in the gospels as places where Jesus is known to come. There, if we wait with prayer and earnest heart, Christ who comes to us in every season of life will come to us creating belief and shining the light of eternal life in our hearts. He will, in his time, take all the substance out of the burial cloths until we need visit them no longer. Christ will set us free to live in new life. He will turn our tears to joy. Jesus will indeed be faithful to do this.

Lord Jesus we believe, help our unbelief. As you came to Mary at the place of her tears, so come to us. Raise our expectations. Clear our sight. Grant us to see that the graveclothes of old wounds and guilts are empty now. Turn us from fear and grief. Show us yourself that we may declare the joy of the truth: You are Lord and Christ. Amen.

Endnote

1. Robert Penn Warren, "Chthonian Revelation" from *Rumor Verified*, (New York: Random House, 1980).

CHAPTER SIXTEEN

I Am With You Always
Matthew 28:16-20

And surely I am with you always,
to the very end of the age.

Matthew 28:20

When Jesus called her name in the garden by his tomb, Mary must have clung to Jesus as she cried out, "Rabonni!" For Jesus then said to her, "Do not hold on to me, for I have not yet returned to the Father. Go instead to my brothers and tell them, 'I am returning to my Father and your Father, to my God and your God'" (John 20:17). Despite the joy of their reunion, Jesus wanted Mary to deliver a message even more urgent than their moment together. His words were, in fact, news of a greater intimacy than even this physical embrace.

Jesus has achieved for us a union with God heretofore impossible. The Son of God came to us where we are in this world of toil and loss. And he became what we are, taking a body that grew tired, felt pain and wrestled with temptation as we do. In short, he took our humanity into himself. On the cross, he took our sins upon himself as well, and they crushed him unto death. But in the eternal power of the love of God, Christ rose. Sin and death were defeated. Jesus came out from the tomb still wearing our humanity, though now it was remade and set free from the ravages of evil and decay. A new human being was in the world, a second Adam, representing a new and better beginning. And the wonder of Christianity is that we may now enter that new life as well.

Paul wrote of this mystery, "For Christ's love compels us, because we are convinced that one died for all, and therefore all died. And he died for all, that those who live should no longer live for themselves but for him who died for them and was raised again ... Therefore, if anyone is in Christ, he is a new creation; the old has gone, the new has come!" (II Cor. 5:14-17). Somehow, some way, by the grace of God, what happened to Jesus in our humanity has happened to us who are united to him. We have died to sin and been given new, resurrection life.

I am returning to my Father and your Father, to my God and your God. Without Christ, we are cut off from the Father and can hardly fathom, let alone embrace the intimacy of such a name for God. But in Christ, we participate in the relationship he has with the Father. We are taken into that fellowship. Jesus' Father is our Father. His God, his relationship with God as a human being, is ours. The God who comes to us in every hour invites us to participate in all he has. We partake *vicariously*, in his life, death, and resurrection, as if what happened to him has happened to us.

Such intimacy, though, occurs in the context of Jesus' saying that he is returning to his Father and our Father. Jesus' ascension into heaven is the completing step that makes all the benefits of his life among us available now. In fact, the doctrine of the ascension, so seldom discussed in our churches, actually provides the gateway through which we may understand how we participate in the Triune life of God through the work of Jesus Christ. The ascension provides the key to understanding how we may partake most fully of the Christ we have met in these stories from the gospels. Perhaps an example from daily life may provide insight into this mystery.

One on behalf of another

I once went to a concert without actually being there. For years I have had a great love for the Irish singer Van Morrison. His music nourishes my soul, and when I am running on empty, under stress, or just full of the passion of life, I often put on one of my two dozen Van Morrison CD's. His version of "Be Thou My Vision" is so hearty it would please St. Patrick himself. Strangely, two of my best friends in the world also find a soul mate in Morrison's music.

Several summers ago, one of these men, Cary, came to visit us on holiday in the North Carolina mountains. That first evening, after dinner he said he had a story he wanted to tell me. He couldn't have told it over the phone; it had to wait to be told in person. Then he handed me a T-shirt – it was from the Van Morrison tour. "You were there," Cary said. And then he told me how it happened.

Van doesn't play a lot of concerts, and he rarely visits more than a handful of cities when he does tour. Sometimes we speculate about where he might be after a new album is released. Cary, who lives in Cincinnati, Ohio, had called a ticket company in New York City, just on a whim. "Yes," the voice said, "Van's playing next Sunday night on the New Jersey shore."

My friend thought instantly of getting tickets and then challenging us to find a way to get there. "But it's sold out," the operator said. "Are you sure?" he asked, "Could you check again?" The agent punched her computer. "I've got one seat."

Van was playing more than four hundred miles away. The concert was on a Sunday night and Cary is a minister. So at noon, right after services, he bolted from the church door in his robes, changing as he drove. Stopping only for fuel, he arrived at the 8:00 p.m. concert an hour late. But Van had been delayed, and the music had just begun. His one ticket was on the twelfth row. The concert was incredible. And as he talked, I knew, I was there.

Cary went without telling either friend. He went, though, in our name and on our behalf. He wasn't alone. And I felt like I had been there. I wanted every detail. It was my trip, vicariously, as much as his. And I had the T-shirt to prove it. My man, my friend had gone up for me.

I don't know if you've ever had such a vicarious experience before. You may not even believe me when I tell you there was a mystical quality about hearing his story. I lived through him. If you've known such a feeling in even a modest way, though, then you are on the way to the meaning of the ascension.

The ascension

Though few of us consider the life of Jesus much beyond Easter, a storyteller or filmmaker would realize right away that there's a dramatic problem. This man, who was somehow God and man, gets killed. But then he lives again. His body comes back to life, and he's walking around. But then how does the story end? Does he just fade away? Or die again, like Lazarus? That would take all the power from the resurrection. The scriptures tell us that Jesus, after forty days of resurrected life among us, ascended up into heaven. The book of Acts paints a picture of him rising into the sky until he was covered by a cloud, and gone. Hollywood could wrap the story with some dazzling special effects.

And perhaps many of us think of the ascension as a kind of dramatic device to explain the unexplainable. Jesus beams up to heaven. It's fantastic, and mysterious, and we'd like to leave it at that. But our natural questions along a literal line actually open up the deep meaning of the ascension. Where is the body of Jesus? Jesus was God incarnate, in the flesh. He took on our humanity. What happened to that human body? Did the union of God and man just dissolve after he left the earth? Did it all just become something spiritual, to be understood only symbolically?

John Knox took the story straight and wrote in the Scots Confession:

> We do not doubt but that the selfsame body which was born of the virgin, was crucified, dead and buried, and which did rise again, did ascend into the heavens, for the accomplishment of all things, where in our name and for our comfort he has received all power in heaven and earth, where he sits at the right hand of the Father ... the only advocate and mediator for us.

That "selfsame body which was born" ascended into the heavens. There, "in our name and for our comfort" he intercedes for us at the right hand of God.

This is, to our contemporary minds, wild stuff: the union of God and man in Jesus Christ continues forever. His body is a resurrection body, it is not subject to decay, but he retains his essential humanity. The Son of God is still, even now, fully human and fully divine. This is not mere symbol and metaphor, but real. And the implications for our lives are staggering.

Jesus, as we noted, is the new Adam, a new creation. He is the Head, the representative, of restored and redeemed humanity. When we as Christ's body are joined to the Head, we are joined to his new humanity, and also become new creatures.

The ascension of Christ is a crucial part of our redemption. The enacting of our salvation began when Jesus, in accordance with the Father's eternal plan, assumed our nature in the first moment of incarnation. It flourished as he lived his life healing and cleansing, loving and obeying. All we have considered in this book shows Jesus among us bringing his salvation. Our redemption reached its climax in Christ's death on the cross for our sins and his rising from the dead for our eternal life. It continues now in his ascending. For Jesus, who took our humanity into himself, takes our humanity, literally, up into the presence of God.

Of course we don't consider that heaven is a place in this dimension that we could reach if we had the right conveyance. Heaven is the realm where God is, where his universal presence is most clearly perceived. That we call it spiritual does not diminish its realness. Quite the contrary; heaven is a realm of reality deeper and truer than we can apprehend.

Jesus entered this heavenly realm still bearing our creaturely humanity, albeit transformed through the resurrection. Now, at the throne of the Father, the Son appears in our name and on our behalf. He is our advocate as well as our Lord, our intercessor as well as the one who hears our prayers.

Moreover, it is the ascended Christ who sends down God the Holy Spirit into the hearts of the disciples. Peter explained the sequence of events in his first sermon. He preached, "God has raised this Jesus to life, and we are all witnesses of the fact. Exalted to the right hand of God, he has received from the Father the promised Holy Spirit and has poured out what you now see and hear ..." (Acts 2:32-33). In ascending, Jesus withdrew physically from his people. But from his place of exaltation, he sends the Holy Spirit to us. As Paul wrote, "God has poured out his love into our hearts by the Holy Spirit whom he has given us" (Rom. 5:5). The Spirit teaches us who Christ is and even prays within us. When we cry out "Abba, Father" to God, it is the Holy Spirit within us who is bearing witness with our spirits that we are the Father's own children (Rom. 8:15-16). So by leaving us in the body, Christ has actually drawn us closer to himself. For he has sent the Holy Spirit who unites us to himself, and lifts us up, spiritually, to where he is, still working on our behalf. The Spirit now empowers our life in Christ.

To return to our example, my friend Cary sat in the twelfth row of a Van Morrison concert, and in some sense, he took me with him. He went as my friend and representative. But my vicarious attendance was only a shadow of reality. Jesus Christ, as the Head of humanity, ascended to his Father, in reality, in the flesh. Joined to Christ by the Holy Spirit through faith, you and I are there with him. Spiritually, we participate now in what Christ has accomplished in his resurrection body. This union is a foretaste of all that will come to us in the future. Paul tells us, "God raised us up in Christ and seated us with him in the heavenly realms in Christ Jesus" (Eph. 2:6). Not only did God come to where we are in Christ, but he has taken us up to be where he is! Christ wants us with him always and he has made it possible.

Appearing on our behalf

We read in the book of Hebrews "Christ entered heaven itself, now to appear for us in God's presence" (Heb. 9:24). Jesus is with his Father now, not only as the beloved Son, but also as our brother and friend. In fact, Jesus does a dual work in the present as he did in his days among us. First he comes to us as God, in the name of God to show us what the loving Father is like. He presents God to us. Hebrews expresses this through an Old Testament quotation spoken by the ascended Christ. Jesus says, "I will declare your name to my brothers; in the presence of the congregation, I will sing your praises" (Heb. 2:12). Through the

Holy Spirit, we begin to see who Jesus is as we study the Scriptures, pray and worship. And as we noted way back in Chapter Two, when we see Jesus, we are seeing who the Father is.

Secondly, though, Jesus comes to his Father as a man, offering obedience and praise on our behalf. Jesus declares, "Here am I, and the children God has given me" (Heb. 2:13). The ascended Christ presents not only himself at the completion of his obedient life on earth, but he presents us along with him. We get included in his righteousness, his faithfulness, his worship, his prayers. Jesus now appears before God on our behalf. As a man, he offers perfect obedience, which we cannot live, on our behalf. Still incarnate, he offers worship in our place. He prays for us as the Son of God but also as a human being. Hebrews goes on to tell us that he ever lives to intercede for us (Heb. 7:25). Jesus ascended. He left the earth. But he didn't stop working. He continues to live and work and pray and worship on our behalf, so that when we are united to him, we are drawn into the very communion of God himself.

Perhaps through such a study as we have undertaken in this book, we feel that we want to live as God desires. We want Christ to be with us always. We want to be part of the new humanity, restored, forgiven, empowered. But looking at our lives, we see the old Adam. We see the sinful nature. We see ourselves doing what we don't want to do, and failing to do what we want to do. Christ may be with us, but we turn so often from being with him. It may seem hopeless. We'll never get it right. And the more we look at ourselves the worse it gets.

Even the great saint Paul cried out, "What a wretched man I am! Who will save me from this body of death?" (Rom. 7:24). And the answer came to him as it does to us. We must stop looking at ourselves and look to Jesus. He has ascended to heaven, having fulfilled all obedience and worship on our behalf and in our name. So Paul cries out, "Thanks be to God through Jesus Christ our Lord!" (Rom. 7:25).

We all drown in the dark pool of self if we gaze in it too long. Look to Jesus. Look at the new Adam. He has passed through hell and gone to heaven. He is there now, in our name. My man is there. My friend has taken the trip for me. He has opened the way for me to be part of what he has done. I am, mystically, seated in the heavenlies with him. Faith, quickened by the Spirit, sees Jesus there and embraces our place with Christ and in Christ.

Returning the favor

A year after the Van Morrison concert, an opportunity arose for me to take Cary vicariously on a journey with me. Cary is of Scottish descent, and his aunt in particular always sees something of the highlander in him. She reminds him of his heritage and talks to him of the hills and crags. For years he has longed to climb those munros.

My wife and I were in Scotland, traveling with some friends past Glen Coe, the dramatic peak of many legends. I felt the mountains calling in a powerful way. When at last we stopped to hike, near the village of Kinlochleven, a strong impulse took over within me. I strode ahead of the others, energy surging. I looked at the distant peak, and thought, "I have to go up there and make my prayers." Joy filled me as I looked down to the narrow loch, and out to the sea now glowing with late summer sun. Across the chasm, the light lit the mountains. Still a peak was above me, and I had to climb. But as I went, though I had physically left the others, I realized I wasn't alone. Cary was with me. Clearly, strongly, I carried his presence into the hills. As strange as it sounds, I felt as if I was there in his name as well as mine.

Months later, when I told him the story, he did not listen as people often politely do to other people's long travel tales. He didn't strain to keep his attention. He was there. He asked for every detail I could remember. He understood. His man had ascended the highland hill on his behalf, and he was there.

Again, such a story is a shadow of reality. But in truth, our man, Christ Jesus, has ascended the heights of heaven for us He still bears his humanity fully, and that means he still bears us with him. You are there, in him. Our friend and brother Jesus, flesh of our flesh and bone of our bones, the new Adam, has ascended, and we went with him. Spiritually for now, yes, but nonetheless in reality.

And we are there. In his famous hymn, "A Mighty Fortress," Luther wrote, "Were not the right man on our side, our striving would be losing." Thankfully, the right man is on our side. Our man has gone up to heaven for us. Our man, our friend and brother, is at God's right hand in our name and on our behalf. Jesus who came to be with us has taken us, spiritually, to be with him. This is the foretaste of the day Jesus spoke of when he said, "And if I go and prepare a place for you, I will come back, and take you to be with me that you may be where I am" (John 14:3). He desires us to be with him always. God wants us with him so much that he came and got us, taking our flesh and humanity back to heaven, uniting us more and more to himself through the Holy Spirit, and promising that at the last we will be fully together. This is the wonderful comfort within the story of the ascension. We are in Christ, seated, not just on the twelfth row of a Van Morrison concert, but in the heavenly places with God.

Go into the world

Finally, all of the gospels conclude with some form of commission for the disciples. In Mark, Jesus says, "Go into all the world and preach the good news to all creation" (Mark 16:15). He tells Peter at the conclusion of John to "Feed my sheep" (John 21:17). In Luke he reminds them to preach "repentance and forgiveness in his name" as witnesses of all they have seen (Luke 24:48). And in the passage from Matthew that contains the title of this book, Jesus says,

> All authority in heaven and on earth has been given to me. Therefore go and make disciples of all nations, baptizing them in the name of the Father and of the Son and of the Holy Spirit, and teaching them to obey everything I have commanded you. And surely I am with you always, to the very end of the age. (Matt. 28:18-20)

We who have seen Christ come to us in every season of life are asked to bear witness to the fact. When we have found the rest for our souls that is in Christ, we are sent to show others how they may enter that peace as well. Our Lord has been exalted to a position of authority above heaven and earth. We serve the reigning king who will come again in splendor. There are wonderful stories to be told, and a gospel to be presented.

Jesus' final words of comfort in Matthew come in the context of his disciples going out into their daily lives with the offer of Christ's love in their hands and his grace on their lips. They are sent to teach what they have been taught, to bring the news to all nations. As they go, they will experience the fullness of his words, "I am with you always."

Day by day, we may locate ourselves in the stories we have considered. We discover through prayer and faith how Christ comes to us now as he did to the people in the gospel accounts. And so we learn the wonderful truth that there is no place God will not go to retrieve us. There is no depth to which he will not stoop to find us. Wherever his lost and wandering children have gone, he goes. In every season and hour of life, he is there. God has come for us in Christ Jesus. The good news of the gospel is that he is with us, forgiving our sins and creating new life within us. Even more, though, we have seen that we are with him. Our true life is found in his humanity. He is not only with us, but has raised us up with him to be in close communion with God. His Father is now our Father. So we find vivid life, genuine peace, deep rest and fullness of joy in Christ Jesus our Lord, he who came to us in the flesh, was crucified, risen, ascended, and is most certainly coming again.

———————•——

Blessed Jesus, thank you for coming to be with us, and even more, for coming to be one of us. We stand amazed at your love. Your incarnation was not temporary but eternal! How could you ever want to be joined always to the likes of us! Yet we would not deny your love because it surpasses our comprehension. Rather we would accept such grace and take our place with you. By faith, we see that you are with us and we are with you. How glorious: we are in you, always. With thanks we pray, Amen.